THE COMPLETE OUTDOORSMAN'S HANDBOOK

THE COMPLETE OUTDOORSMAN'S HANDBOOK

A Guide to Outdoor Living and Wilderness Survival

JEROME J. KNAP

PAGURIAN PRESS LIMITED

TORONTO

Printed and Bound in Canada
Library of Congress Catalog Card Number: 74-79519
ISBN 0-919364-62-4

Distributed in the United States by:
Arco Publishing Company, Inc.
219 Park Avenue South
New York, N.Y. 10003

Arco Book Ordering Number: 3514

COPY 1

OTHER BOOKS BY JEROME J. KNAP

The Canadian Hunter's Handbook

101 Tips to Improve Your Fishing

The Hunter's Handbook

Training the Versatile Gun Dog (with Alyson Knap)

Getting Hooked on Fishing (with David Richey)

Where to Fish and Hunt in North America

ACKNOWLEDGMENTS AND PICTURE CREDITS

My most sincere thanks to E. B. Sanders for his many fine pen-and-ink sketches which illustrate this book.

Thanks are also due to the following persons and organizations for the use of photographs: Arkansas Fish and Game Commission (page 158); Bausch and Lomb Incorporated (page 66); Buck Knives Incorporated (pages 68 and 77); Bushnell Optical Incorporated (page 64); Canadian Government Travel Bureau (page 28); Gerry/Outdoor Sports Industries Incorporated (pages 31 and 99); Jerome Knap (pages 54 and 80); E. Leitz Incorporated (pages 60 and 65); McCulloch Corporation (page 86); Normark Corporation (page 75 and 152); Ontario Ministry of Industry and Tourism (pages 82, 103, 107, 135, 138 and 142); Ontario Ministry of Natural Resources (pages 120 and 131); Outboard Marine Corporation (page 147); Pennsylvania Game Commission (pages 34 and 32); RU-KO of Canada Limited (page 73).

Contents

Introduction

There is an outdoor recreation boom sweeping the entire western world and this continent in particular. There has been nothing like it in the past. Yes, the out-of-doors has always had an appeal for some, but they have been a small minority. Two decades ago you could go on a canoe trip in the summer months in the wilderness of Quetico and not see another soul for an entire week. Not today. You are lucky if you see only three or four canoeing parties a day.

Arctic rivers that have not seen a white man's canoe since the big fur-trading era, today are being traveled regularly. The old trails of the western mountains, untrodden since the days of mountain men and early prospectors, are being hiked and backpacked today. During the height of summer, camping areas in many parks are full. In the past, being a fishing and hunting outfitter was a risky business. It still is, but today many outfitters in the more popular areas have no difficulty in attracting clientele.

This phenomenon is world-wide. In many of the national parks of Africa, one can see a pride of mini-buses around every lion. I have even met a convoy of two land rovers on safari in the middle of the Kalahari Desert in Botswana.

The reasons for this outdoor boom are many. A greater interest in wildlife is one. Twenty years ago hunters and fishermen were the only large groups interested in wildlife. Today, almost everyone has a casual interest in wild creatures. This interest is not always tempered with wisdom, and is rarely accompanied by knowledge. At times wildlife management agencies are hampered in their work by people who prefer to have deer starve than to have them hunted by outdoorsmen.

Other reasons for the outdoor boom are more leisure time, a more affluent society, and better highways and rapid transportation systems. Thirty years ago, if a New York big-game hunter wanted to hunt in the Yukon, it took him five days just to reach Whitehorse. Today, he is there in less than a day. But I think that the biggest reason for the outdoor boom is a spiritual rebellion against our sophisticated, affluent society. Deep down we hunger for a quieter life, a slower pace, green grass, and the sight of pale blue wood smoke curling up toward the sky. We want to "get away from it all," but at times we bring it all with us in the form of tent cities and slums.

Everyone who ventures into the out-of-doors should possess the basic skills for outdoor living. He should know how to make a good campfire, what types of wood give fast heat for boiling tea, and what types provide hot flames for broiling steaks. He should know how to paddle a canoe, how to forecast weather, how to use a compass, what the sudden cry of a bluejay means, and what a bear is up to when he stands on his hind legs. The average outdoorsman does not have to be a wilderness survival expert, but he should know the basics. After all, almost everyone can become lost or lose his gear when his canoe is upset in a choppy wilderness lake.

The outdoorsman should know all this and much more. He should know about the natural world around him — how it lives and functions. He should know its moods, its sounds, and its signals. But above all, the outdoorsman must have a code, an outdoor ethic, to ensure that his life and travels in the out-of-doors are in harmony with nature. Man, like all creatures, is a user. This is how nature created him. Frequently our use leaves wounds. Every campfire, every hiking trail, every fish caught, and every grouse shot is a wound. But these are wounds that nature heals and repairs with ease. An outdoorsman should never leave wounds that will permanently scar. That is what the outdoor code and the outdoor ethic are all about.

Chapter 1

Understanding the Out-of-Doors

A good outdoorsman is more than just a man who enjoys the out-of-doors and possesses the necessary skills for an outdoor life. The ability to identify that little brown bird on the dogwood branch and know why crows mob on a hardwood ridge are not enough. To be a good outdoorsman a man should know all this, but more important, he must understand how nature around him functions.

Let us imagine that we are high on a ridge overlooking a forested valley. It is apparent that the forest is the dominant factor of all life in the valley. Through the canopy of green, we can see the occasional gray skeleton of a dead tree. As we walk through the valley, we see the forest floor. In places nothing but large trees grow. The floor is covered with leaves from last autumn. In other places, where spots of light penetrate the green blanket over our heads, seedlings and saplings grow, their branches hungrily reaching toward the light. Here and there tree trunks dot the forest floor, their bodies in various stages of decay. Gray skeletons of a few dead trees still stand upright.

Not all the dead trees are big and old. Trees seldom die of old age. They die from competition. As a seedling sprouts, it immediately begins to compete with other seedlings around it for light, nourishment, and moisture. As it grows into a sapling, it competes again against other saplings for the same essential elements. A tree lives as long as it has the strength to endure the competition. It lives as long as it can endure depredations from creatures of all kinds. Insects feed on its tissues; rodents gnaw at its bark; deer browse at its tips. A tree is also host to fungi and bacteria. Creatures and organisms of all kinds use a tree for food and shelter.

The forest and the creatures that live in it are woven together in an intricate web. Rodents that prey on the tree are in turn preyed upon by foxes and owls. Deer that browse the tree tips are preyed upon by wolves, and at times by men. Insects that feed on the tree are preyed upon by birds. And birds that live among the branches of the tree

11

scatter the seeds of trees so that new trees will grow. When a calamity strikes a part of the forest, a portion of that web, its impact reverberates throughout all the other strands of the web.

In what is now a classical study of a forest community, Dr. Arthur Williams conducted population research in a sixty-five acre beech and hard-maple woodlot. The year the study began, the beeches and maples produced bumper crops of fruits, nuts, and samaras. As a result, small mammals were exceedingly abundant in the area. The following summer there was a drought and the crops of nuts and samaras failed. Insect hatches were poor as well.

The impact was catastrophic on the creatures of the woodlot. Gray squirrels declined drastically in number. Many moved out. Chipmunks starved in the winter because they could not store enough food to feed themselves. Their population crashed by ninety percent. The shrews, which are insectivorous, could not find enough insects to feed on; hence they turned to preying on forest mice. Under the onslaught of abnormally heavy predation, the mouse population decreased by eighty percent. As the population of mice declined, the shrew population also dropped by sixty-five percent. Why? They starved.

The failure of the nut and samara crop also had an impact on the larger mammals. In the autumn, the woodlot held about forty cottontails. Two red foxes and several skunks hunted there frequently. The next spring only two rabbits remained. The reason was the lack of mice. The foxes were forced to spend more time hunting cottontails because mice, their usual prey, were reduced to such low levels by the shrews. Skunks, which also prey on mice and on insects, left the woodlot completely.

The following year the maples and beeches produced normal crops of samaras and nuts. Mice, chipmunks, and squirrels increased to their usual numbers. By autumn, there were over fifty rabbits in the woodlot. Why? During the year when the mice and cottontails were reduced in numbers, no animals browsed and gnawed on the twigs and shoots of the brush and the young maples and beeches. Everything grew in profusion. There was a superabundance of food the following year, and the rabbits multiplied.

There is no doubt that similar fluctuations occurred among the birds — seed eaters, insect eaters, and birds of prey. But since birds can move about much more readily, they were less affected than the cottontails, chipmunks, mice, and shrews, who are homebodies,

---

The forest and its creatures live together in an intricate web. Each year ▶
some must die to nourish and make room for others.

12

spending their entire lives in one small "home range".

Although the actions and interactions of the plants and wildlife in this woodlot were under scientific scrutiny, any observant outdoorsman could have made reasonably accurate deductions as to what was happening, the reasons for it, and what might happen in the future. A good outdoorsman understands the outdoor world around him. Long before such biological terms as ecology, habitat, eco-system, carrying capacity, annual turnover, and environment became common usage, many old-time woodsmen knew about them. They did not know the words themselves, indeed they would not have known what they meant, but they knew the happenings behind these terms.

A decade or more ago towards the end of winter I spent a few days with an old French-Canadian trapper. When the talk turned to what kind of a season he had had, he showed me a stack of two-dozen lynx pelts.

"Been getting a few more every year for the past eight or nine years," he said. "But this will be the last good year for them cats. There ain't no rabbits any more and these lynx were kind of poor. Some wasn't very big.

"It'll take the rabbits a few years to come back, and then I'll start getting them cats again," he continued.

The astuteness of his conversation struck me later. I am sure that he never thought of his observations as being particularly noteworthy, but they were. He had summarized not only the essence of a predator-prey relationship, but also an understanding of the complexity of the snowshoe hare-lynx cycle. He knew that as snowshoe hare populations increased in their ten-year cycle, the number of lynx would also increase, but when the snowshoe hare cycle crashed to its low point, the lynx population would also decline, but one year after the hares. The fact that the cats were thin and that some, the young of that year, were somewhat smaller than normal showed that they were undernourished.

Observations and deductions such as these can be made by any-one who understands what is happening around him. A South Dakota pheasant hunter can get a fairly good idea of the kind of fall pheasant season he can expect by remembering the severity of the previous winter and the temperatures and rainfall of the spring that followed it. If the winter had had deep snow, pheasants would have survived only in the best of covers. This means that the breeding population would be lower than average. If the spring had been wet and cold, the size of hatches and survival of pheasant chicks would be poor. Low breeding populations and poor hatches and poor survival of chicks means low populations of pheasants in the fall.

14

In mid-winter, with little snow, pheasants will survive even in marginal covers. A high breeding population in the spring will result. If the spring is favorable, good hatches and high chick survival rates will result. A high breeding population, good hatches, and good survival of chicks will mean a bumper crop of ringnecks in the fall.

Every outdoorsman should understand the basic law of nature — the principle of carrying capacity. The tenets of this law can be seen on almost every outing, even in a city park. If you want to see certain species of wildlife, you go to places where they are abundant. For example, if you want to see a white-tailed deer, you go into a young forest with much brush and sapling growth. The deer here have plenty of browse. Mature forests have low carrying capacity for deer, because tender shoots and branches are too high for the deer to reach. On the other hand, if you want to see wild turkey, you must go to mature forests because only mature forests bear mast for turkeys to feed on.

The main reason why any species of animal is abundant is because the habitat is suitable for its mode of life. In other words, the habitat has the capacity to support that species — to give it food and shelter. But there is more to it than that. The carrying capacity of any habitat is limited. Just as a bridge with a warning sign "Eight-Ton Limit" has a limited carrying capacity, so any given habitat has one as well.

For example, nearly every winter many of the northern Great Lakes states report starvation among deer. This is simply the law of carrying capacity in action. If there are too many deer for the habitat to support, some of the deer must die. This carrying capacity is not static. In a severe winter of deep snows, the carrying capacity is decreased because the deer herds will confine themselves to sheltered areas. Conversely, in mild winters, deer herds spread out and thereby increase the carrying capacity of the forest. Their survival rate in mild winters is high.

Some years ago Missouri biologists carried out a three-year study on bobwhite quail in two areas of the same size holding about the same numbers of quail. In one area all hunting was banned and conservation officers enforced the ban. In the other area hunting was allowed during the normal quail season. At the end of every winter, the bobwhite populations in these two areas proved to be the same. The law of carrying capacity was the reason for this. There was no way that the quail could increase beyond the winter carrying capacity of their range. Nature would not let them. In one way or another, the surplus quail were disposed of.

If a city park has a carrying capacity of fifty robins, every spring you will find not more or less than that number, regardless of the number of young robins that were hatched the previous summer. In lakes, food is frequently the determining factor in carrying capacity. With fish, carrying capacity can be expressed in terms of pounds per acre. If a lake has sufficient food for a thousand largemouth bass to grow to one pound, then two-hundred bass would be able to grow to five pounds each.

Carrying capacities of habitats increase and decrease with time. Forest fires may be devastating when they are burning, but they bring benefits as well. We have made a cult of Smokey the Bear, but in many cases this has been at the expense of wildlife. A forest fire is only temporarily destructive. Any moose-hunting guide in northern Ontario will tell you that the best moose hunting is on old burns, about twenty years after the fire. There is a lot of sapling

---

Trees live only as long as they can endure competition from other trees and depredation from bacteria, fungi, insects, and mammals. But even when a tree dies, it decays and nourishes others.

growth and feed for moose at that time. Indeed, as nature repairs the damage by establishing young forests, a great variety and abundance of wildlife develop in the early stages. Wildlife biologists have recognized this and are now actually burning marginal forests to create better wildlife habitat.

The carrying capacity of most habitats can be increased or decreased. When a farmer decides to clean up a brushy fence row, or clear the fence completely so that his big farm machinery can work more effectively, he is destroying the home of a variety of birds and small mammals. When a marsh is drained or a new expressway is built, the same thing happens. The reason that bluebirds have decreased in numbers in many areas is a by-product of our search for beauty. We have cut down many old hollow trees. Without hollow trees, bluebirds have no place to nest. The list of such cases is endless.

In nature, the life of a single individual is meaningless. For every creature born, one must die. Nature has long ago asserted that two monarch butterflies or two northern pike cannot occupy the same place at the same time. The well attuned outdoorsman recognizes this. He recognizes that life is based on the conversion of carbon atoms from one form to another. He recognizes that energy is released by this conversion. He recognizes that every creature on earth, including man, is a user and a consumer of the carbon atoms. He also recognizes that in our use, we must strive for harmony with nature and the wounds that we leave as a result of our use must heal quickly, without leaving a scar.

Chapter 2

Outdoor Know-How

The Bushmen of the Kalahari Desert teach their sons the skills of hunting — how to stalk and call game, how to understand the tracks of animals and other game signs, the habits and behavior of animals, and everything else about the dry, sparse desert brush around them. The boys learn from childhood. They are taken on hunting forays at a very early age and there is no doubt that experience is a good teacher. It takes mud on your boots and many hours of observation, both in sunny weather and foul, to learn about the habits and ways of wildlife.

But there are other ways of learning many outdoor skills. For example, I have learned to identify many birds without leaving my living room. Two bird feeders outside the window and a bird guide were a great help. One feeder contained seeds for the seed-eating birds, while the other held suet for the insect eaters. In my spare moments, I would watch the birds. Whenever a strange bird visited one of the feeders, I would identify it with the help of the bird guide. Once I learned how to spot their key identifying features and learned to recognize the more common ones, I was ready for the birds in woodlots and wilderness areas.

One can learn a great many outdoor skills from books. Indeed, this is one of the reasons for writing this one. I don't mean to imply that books are a substitute for actual experience. They can't do that, but they can give you the basic instructions — a foundation that will make the learning process in the field much easier. They can save you time, money, and mistakes. From books, you can learn the basics of using a compass, sharpening a knife, choosing a canoe, setting a

---

◀ *A bluejay constantly calling from the same area probably indicates that it has spotted a predator, perhaps a fox. The bluejay is boldly announcing the predator's presence.*

snare or trap, identifying tracks, or identifying wild plants, whether edible or poisonous. The list is endless. Once you know the basics, experience will give you proficiency. None of us has enough time to learn all these skills by trial and error and learning solely by experience is a matter of trial and error.

Aside from books, instruction from someone who knows is another way to knowledge. In many cases teachers are superior to books. Learning how to cast with a fly rod is much easier with proper instruction than reading a dozen chapters on casting in a dozen fly-fishing books. The same can be said about paddling a canoe, sharpening a knife, and a host of other things. There is no doubt that an experienced, skillful partner from whom one can learn is an invaluable asset.

Phonograph records and tapes can be used to learn how to call ducks, geese, and crows, or how to imitate the plaintive distress call of a rabbit, which will attract such predators as foxes and coyotes. Recorded bird songs are an excellent way to learn to identify the songs of birds.

However, there are things that books and people can explain, but never really teach. To become a good outdoorsman, one needs exposure to the out-of-doors, but one also needs some basic aptitudes — keen powers of observation and an alert mind capable of rational and logical thinking. Unfortunately not everyone possesses these traits. Some people never learn to think or to see beyond the obvious. With many people it is not a question of ability, but of concentration. A business executive going on a weekend backpacking trip will not think beyond the obvious if he is subconsciously thinking about a Monday morning sales meeting. Our way of life, our society, frequently makes such strong demands on us that we cannot divorce ourselves from them and immerse ourselves completely in our recreational pursuits.

I learned at an early age that a flock of crows cawing angrily and milling about meant that they had an owl or a hawk up a tree. Birds of prey, particularly the great horned owl, are traditional enemies of crows. If you are a bird watcher, coming across a group of angry crows like this could mean an opportunity to see a hawk or an owl.

A bluejay calling from the same spot probably indicates that it has spotted some predator, perhaps a fox, and is boldly scolding the predator and announcing its presence. The bluejay will also call when it sees you slipping through the woods. I doubt if there is a deer hunter around whose presence has not been broadcast by a bluejay.

When a beaver far down the lake slaps his tail on the water and dives under, it means only one thing — something has frightened it. It may have been a fisherman, but if you are deep in the bush where few people travel, it could have been something else. I saw my first pack of timber wolves, a bitch with several half grown cubs, under exactly this kind of circumstance. I had stopped fishing for a moment to see what was alarming the beaver, when suddenly the wolves emerged from the woods and began walking along the shore. They passed across a small bay, no more than 120 yards from me. Since that time, I have seen other wolves, black bear, moose, and deer under similar circumstances.

TRAINING YOUR SENSES

There is no question that our life styles have dulled our sense of sight, hearing, and very probably smell as well. It is not that our eyes

---

When a beaver far down the lake slaps its tail on the water and dives under, it means only one thing. Something has frightened it.

are less sharp or our hearing less keen than those of our ancestors, but we don't use our eyes or our ears in the same way.

Eight or nine years ago I took a city friend moose hunting — his first moose hunt. Before dawn the first morning we walked to a beaver meadow and sat down on a high ridge. As the first arrows of light hurled themselves across the yellow grass, we began glassing the meadow for moose.

"There's nothing there," my partner said almost out loud.

"I wouldn't say that. I see a cow with two calves," I whispered.

"Where?"

"Over that clump of spruce. Those moose are just inside the bush."

My partner focused his binoculars on the spot I had indicated, but still could not see the moose. They blended fairly well with the dark spruce, but to me, they were not all that inconspicuous. What gave them away were their backs — the only horizontal lines among a mass of vertical ones. Not until one of the calves moved was my partner able to pick them out. Looking for horizontal lines in a forest is one of the first tricks I learned in the outdoors. Sure I see a great many fallen logs and rocks, but I also see game which would otherwise escape my notice.

Another thing I learned early is never to look for an entire animal. You will seldom ever see one in a bush until you have waited it out and it steps into the open. If you want to see a squirrel on a high oak, don't look for a squirrel. Rather look for the tip of a tail, the odd corner of a head sticking out, or a bump on a branch that may be the bushytail's back, and so on.

You must also learn where to look. This requires a fair amount of knowledge about the habitats of animals. Don't expect to see a goshawk sitting high in the top branches of a dead elm. Generally goshawks sit in the middle branches and nearly always in live trees that offer some cover. They prefer to sit on the edges of clearings, not outside, but only a little way into the bush.

Similarly, you will seldom see an old buck deer walking out in the open in broad daylight. The only time he will be in the open is at dusk or dawn when something has really scared him, but then he will be running. Big old bucks prefer to travel in some cover — just inside the tree line, by a brushy fence row, or along a wooded ridge. That is where you should be looking. Incidentally, foxes usually behave in the same way. A fox may lie down in an open field to sun itself, but it will have gone there at dawn. Once it's there, it will stay there, relying on stillness and camouflage for protection, unless someone or something frightens it.

One of the things that separates a seasoned woodsman from a beginner is the ability to interpret signs. An experienced outdoorsman

22

makes a mental note of everything he sees — a track, a clump of droppings, a rub mark, or a claw mark on a tree. Once a partner of mine and I were hiking up a steep portage trail. I lugged the canoe while he carried our gear and fishing tackle. We were going to fish a small lake on a high hill. As we labored up the path, we came across a pile of bear dung. Our talk turned to bears.

"You know," my partner said, "I've never seen a bear in the bush except in the big national parks out west, and those roadside bears can hardly be considered wild."

"I can probably show you one today," I replied.

"That's kind of a tall statement," my partner answered.

It was obvious that he was more than skeptical about my claim. I said nothing. Coming back late that afternoon I put the canoe down at a sharp ridge and told my partner to leave the gear beside it. I dug out a pair of small binoculars from my packsack and told my partner to follow me quietly. I knew the country well. About half a mile from the trail, the hill became a gentle slope. A forest fire had burned over the slope twenty or more years ago. The new trees were in the sapling stage of growth and included several big clumps of wild cherries. There was a good chance that a bear would be feeding on the cherries.

My hunch was right. In fact, there were four bears. We watched them for a while until we were afraid that darkness would overtake us if we didn't leave.

"How did you know the bears would be there?" my partner asked when we got back to our canoe and gear.

"Oh, I put two and two together," I replied. "There were cherry pits in the bear dung. I knew that this slope had wild cherries on it because I hunted grouse here a couple of years ago. And bears are generally more active in the mornings and evenings during the summer months, so they would most likely be at the cherries in the late afternoon or early morning."

SOUNDS AND SMELLS

Learning to recognize sounds is equally important to learning to see and interpret signs. Generally our ears are attuned to the mechanical sounds that are such a large part of our world, but every bird or mammal emits a sound of some sort as well. So do fish, amphibians, reptiles, and insects.

There is no doubt as to what the buzzing of a rattle on a rattlesnake means. But first you must be able to identify the sound. I've known people who lived in country where rattlesnakes were common and who ventured outdoors regularly, but who did not know how a rattlesnake sounded. That kind of ignorance could cost them their lives.

Learning to identify wildlife sounds is a facet of outdoorsmanship, but it is equally important to learn what the sounds mean. The chatter of a red squirrel as it scampers about unconcerned has a specific tone. That tone completely changes when the squirrel spots potential danger.

Once I actually saw a fisher chase a red squirrel through the tree-tops. What alerted me to this was the hysterical chatter before the chase started. Once the fisher was in pursuit, the squirrel stopped its chatter. It was too busy running for its life.

I am certain that crows possess the most developed language of all birds. I like crows. They may be rogues, but they are not as black as they are sometimes painted. When I was a kid on the family farm, I spent much of my spare time trying to outwit these sly birds as they gorged themselves on freshly planted corn. Mind you, I learned the futility of this early, but it was always a good excuse for roaming in the woodlot. That is how crows earned my everlasting admiration. They seemed to possess a sound for almost every situation and more than one for a boy with a shotgun.

Our sense of smell has also been blunted, probably by constant exposure to automobile exhausts, outboard motors, dust, and smoke of all kinds, including cigarettes. I have noticed that when I have been away from the city in the wilderness for a week or two, my sense of smell becomes much sharper. I can detect odors that would normally remain hidden.

Man, or any primate for that matter, is not known for his olfactory powers. But my association with the pre-literate tribes of Africa has shown me that these people do possess a better sense of smell than we do. No doubt once industrialization catches up with them, they too will lose it.

However, our sense of smell does allow us to enjoy the outdoors more — the fragrance of flowers, the pleasant but pungent odor of humus and moss, the sharp smell of cedar, and the sweet smell of pine. But at times it is possible to smell more than that. A bull elk in rut has a very strong odor. I once knew a big-game guide who could smell elk before he could see them. Big rattlesnakes also exude a strong, goat-like smell when angry. Bears sometimes emit strong odors. At times I have smelled bear long before seeing their fresh tracks in soft earth. These odors are so distinctive that once they are identified, you will never forget them.

As I write this, my favorite dog is curled up at my feet underneath my desk. This is her favorite spot when I am working. I have often wondered what it would be like to have a sense of smell like hers. She can point a ruffed grouse at thirty yards or farther.

INTERPRETING ANIMAL ACTIONS

Interpreting the actions of birds and mammals is something that can be learned only by observing them. Once while on a canoe trip in northern Manitoba, I met a young couple on an island campsite. Our talk eventually turned to blueberries. The young woman expressed great interest in picking some. The three of us paddled across to the mainland and climbed a steep hill to look for a blueberry patch. We found one, but a black bear in the brown-color phase that is common in western Canada, had found it first.

The bear greeted our intrusion by standing up.

"He's going to charge!" the man injected fearfully. With this, the bear dropped onto its four feet and with a loud "whoof " bounded into the bush.

"What made you think he was going to charge?" I asked incredulously.

"When I saw him stand, I thought we were in trouble," the young man said.

"Bears standing on their hind legs charge only in wood cuts of old books and calendars," I answered. The bear had stood up to have a better look at us. He was trying to figure out what we were. Bears have very poor eyesight. When a bear charges, he comes on all fours. That is the only way he can run fast. In a really determined charge, his mouth is wide open and his lips are in full snarl. He is likely to roar when he begins the charge. And, of course, the only bear that will charge a man unprovoked is a grizzly or a polar bear.

Almost everyone knows that to approach big game you must have the wind in your favor — blowing into your face or at least across your face. But there are other things to consider as well. Wild sheep and pronghorns have extremely good eyesight. A man appearing against a skyline will frighten both species. If you want to get close to a bighorn or a pronghorn, walk below the ridge top, stealing only peeks over the hilltop. Sheep are generally easier to approach from above. They don't seem to be as watchful in that direction, probably because potential predators such as wolves, cougars, or bears generally approach from below. Get above the sheep if you want to have a closer look or if you want to get within camera range.

If you want to see big game, pay close attention to thermal breezes. As the air heats and cools in hilly, rolling country, it causes thermal breezes. At times these breezes are so gentle and faint that you may not notice them. In the morning, when the sun's early rays hit the side of a mountain that has been cool all night, the air at the lower elevation warms up and gently flows uphill. In the late afternoon, when the hillside becomes dark, the reverse happens and the thermal breeze flows downward.

To someone out for a stroll, thermal breezes mean nothing. But if you are hunting big game — with a camera or a rifle — these breezes become important. They can carry a warning scent from you to the animal, spooking it before you can even get close.

Chapter 3

Wildlife Hazards

The western mountains are a spectacular sight, but a mountain slope without wild sheep is just a landscape. It is wildlife that makes landscapes come alive. There is no doubt that wildlife is one of the big attractions, one of the main reasons why people venture into the out-of-doors.

Yet there are times when some species can prove to be something of a nuisance, or even a hazard. For example, I have had porcupines chew up my ax handles and canoe paddles. Of course, the porkies were after the salt on the handles from the sweat off my hands. I have also had raccoons raid my food supplies, and even chipmunks and mice will nibble holes in cardboard food boxes to get at the contents. I have even had mink steal my fish. These nuisances are easy to cope with. In most cases the damage is due to the outdoorsman's carelessness. On canoe trips I hang my food when asleep or when I am away from camp. When camping with an automobile, I lock my food in a metal ice chest or wooden box. I now keep my ax and canoe paddles by my side when asleep, or in a tent when I am away. And I have never minded sharing my catch with a mink, particularly if I can get a look at this attractive little fur-bearer.

However, every outdoorsman must recognize that there are species of wildlife that are potentially dangerous. All bears are potentially dangerous, particularly females with young, and bears that just feel threatened. Bull moose during the rutting season have been known to be cantankerous. All small carnivores — foxes, coyotes, skunks, and raccoons, in particular — are potential rabies carriers. Of course everyone realizes that poisonous snakes are dangerous. Porcupines are dangerous to dogs. But most dangerous of all are big-game animals on roads and highways. There are ways to cope with all these potential hazards.

BEARS

All bears can be dangerous. The black bear seldom presents any real hazard. Sows with cubs have attacked people when they believed that the cubs were threatened, but unprovoked attacks are extremely rare. Black bears can be a nuisance. I have had black bears raid my food supplies and even break into my tent. I have had them steal moose meat from me. Black bears raid garbage containers and "panhandle" in many of the national parks. These half-tame bears are very dangerous because they have no natural fear of humans. I remember one particularly stupid incident of a black bear badly mauling a woman tourist. The woman was feeding the bear cookies while her husband was filming the event, but the woman ran out of

---

All bears can be dangerous. Grizzlies in particular have been known to attack unprovoked.

cookies and the bear became angry because his supply of cookies had suddenly been cut off.

Grizzly bears (and in this I include the big Alaskan brown bear) and polar bears are much more dangerous and more aggressive than black bears. They are also much bigger and much stronger. The polar bear is dangerous because he seldom, if ever, comes into contact with humans. Polar bears have actually come up to people from a great distance.

Grizzlies attack people with some regularity. The grizzly has been known to attack completely unprovoked. Some years ago one grizzly killed two young women in one of the big national parks while they were asleep in their sleeping bags.

Sows with cubs are more prone to attack than lone bears. If you ever accidentally come between a sow grizzly and her cubs, she will attack. But a grizzly at a food site, such as a winter-starved elk, is also dangerous. If the bear thinks that you are out there to steal his food, he may come at you. More than one big-game hunter has been charged by a grizzly that claimed the hunter's kill.

Of course a wounded grizzly is very dangerous. If he gets away into thick cover, the deck becomes vastly stacked in his favor. I figure there is better than a fifty-fifty chance that the hunter will be mauled or killed.

Both polar bears and grizzlies will also raid food caches if they come across them. But they are not the raiders that the black bear is. This may be because they are not as numerous as black bears and because they live in areas where large numbers of people never venture.

No one should venture into bear country without being observant. If you see a bear, give him a wide berth. Go ahead and watch him, but from a safe distance with binoculars. When traveling in the grizzly country of the western states, western Canada, and Alaska, I would use binoculars to glass the countryside whenever possible before walking through it.

If the cover is too thick, make a noise as you walk — talk, sing, whistle. Some hikers carry tin cans filled with pebbles to rattle. Nearly every bear will run if he gets a chance, if he's warned that a human is present. When walking in thick cover, as on a forest trail, look at the trail for grizzly tracks. If fresh tracks are present, be extra cautious. Both grizzly and black bears have very poor eyesight. Their senses of smell and hearing are excellent, perhaps better than that of a white-tailed deer or an elk.

Bears nearly always begin their charge with a roar. There is no mistaking their intention. Their lips are furled and their jaws are wide open. Incidentally, the old trick of playing dead when being

29

mauled by a bear seems to work. There are a number of incidents when this has saved the victim's life.

The fact that bears can be dangerous should not deter anyone from venturing into bear country. If you exhibit a trace of caution and common sense, you will be in no danger. Walking across the average city street presents greater danger than hiking in bear country.

OTHER WILD LIFE

Deer, elk, caribou, moose, wild sheep, mountain goats, bison, cougars, and wolves present no danger. They are all very fearful of man. Cougars and wolves have been known to follow people, but this seems to be largely due to curiosity. Actual attacks are rare. There are only two or three cougar attacks on record. Similarly, there are very few wolf attacks on record and there is a strong probability that the attacking wolves were rabid. Bull moose during the rutting season have been known to chase people, to attack horses, and even to attack automobiles and trains. But such incidents are very rare. Bull moose in rut sometimes do unusual things, but I can recall doing unusual things when I was amorously chasing some young maiden.

RABIES

The incidence of rabies has increased dramatically in recent years. This may be a cyclic sort of phenomenon or because the numbers of small carnivorous animals have increased and there is a larger pool for the virus. The reason why we have more coyotes, foxes, skunks, and raccoons is twofold: first, our farmers and agriculture departments have become more enlightened and no longer hire poisoners to kill these creatures and, second, few men earn a living as fur trappers any more. There are easier and more comfortable ways to earn one's daily bacon and beans.

A rabid animal is a dangerous one. The most common symptom of rabies is unusual behavior; for example, a fox running toward you rather than away from you or acting sick and stupid. If you encounter such an animal, stay away from it. Keep your kids and dogs away from it. If you have a firearm, shoot the animal, but not through the head. You don't want to damage the brain. A veterinarian will need a section from the brain to determine if the animal was rabid or just acting strangely without any apparent motive.

If anyone is bitten by a wild animal, he should see a doctor immediately. It is even more important then to kill the animal that did the biting, so that it can be diagnosed for rabies. If the doctor cannot learn whether the animal was rabid, he will have to assume that it was and begin a series of anti-rabies injections. If your dogs go with you on outdoor rambles, they should be vaccinated against rabies and receive proper boosters regularly.

DEQUILLING A DOG

For some reason, many dogs don't like porcupines. Maybe it is because the slow, dull-witted porky seems helpless. When a dog rushes

---

If your dog goes with you on outdoor rambles, be sure that he is vaccinated against rabies and receives adequate boosters regularly.

in to attack he, of course, gets an unpleasant surprise. Embedded quills are dangerous if not removed soon. They will work into the dog, causing pain, infection, and possibly even death if they hit vital organs. If you are near a vet, get your dog to him right away. The vet will anesthetize the dog and remove the quills. If you are on a wilderness trip, you will have to dequill the dog yourself.

To do this, you will have to have someone hold the dog still or, if a second person is not available, you will have to tie the dog. The best way to do this is to wrap a jacket or blanket around the dog and tie it with a rope or belt so that the dog cannot hit you with his feet. Twist out each quill slowly with a pair of needle-nosed pliers,

Although deer are the most frequent victims of automobile collisions, other big-game animals such as elk, moose, and even bears have been hit by cars.

starting in the chest area. Remember that the dog will be frightened and in pain, and may become a fear biter. You may have to use a muzzle or gently tie the dog's mouth closed with a handkerchief or a piece of rope. When you have taken out the quills, get the dog to the veterinarian as soon as possible so that he can get a shot to prevent any secondary infection.

WILDLIFE ON HIGHWAYS

Big-game animals — mostly deer, but sometimes elk, moose, and even bears — are a very real hazard to motorists traveling in big-game country. Some years ago I wrote a story on this for one of the motoring magazines. To document my story, I obtained statistics from states known for their vast deer herds. My findings surprised me. In one year, the relatively small state of Pennsylvania alone, reported 22,610 automobile collisions with deer. Texas reported 16,145; California, 8517; and Michigan, 7077, just to name a few. The province of Ontario reported 153 collisions with moose and 45 with black bears. Many of the moose collisions caused human fatalities.

A motorist in big-game country should drive defensively. You never know when a deer may leap out in front of your car. If you see a deer on the side of a road, slow down. Obey all deer-crossing signs. (They were put there for a purpose.) A deer may be standing in the middle of the road just around the next bend. If an animal is on the road at night, turn your headlights off momentarily, leaving on only your parking lights. The animal may be mesmerized by the beam of light, and the moment of darkness may be enough for it to jump out of the way.

If a collision seems unavoidable, don't try to swerve to miss the animal. You may go into a spin and lose control of the car, hitting something more formidable, such as a rock or a tree. It is best to hit the animal straight on. If a collision does occur, treat it like any other accident and report it to the police. Even if the damage to your car is negligible, report the accident to a conservation officer. If the animal is seriously injured, he will want to track it down to prevent further suffering. He may be able to salvage some of the meat for a charitable institution. He may also want to take biological data from the animal.

Above all, don't go near the stricken animal. Wounded deer have been known to lash out with their hoofs and cause injuries. Wounded moose or bears are even more dangerous. Let a police officer or a conservation officer deal with the animal.

33

SNAKES

Snakes have been feared, vilified, and venerated by man from time immemorial. Generally western cuture has been anti-snake. And even today there are still ignorant people around who kill every snake on sight. But we are slowly becoming more enlightened and are starting to realize that snakes are an interesting group of animals.

Of the two-hundred-plus species of snakes found in the United States and Canada, only a few are poisonous. Many species, even the poisonous ones, are very beneficial in controlling populations of small rodents. However, there is no question that care should be exercised by anyone venturing into the out-of-doors in country where poisonous snakes are common. The outdoorsman should not only be able to recognize poisonous snakes, but should know the type of habitat that they prefer, the precautions to be taken against being bitten, and what to do in case of a snake bite.

There are two families of terrestrial poisonous snakes on this continent — the coral snakes and the pit vipers. The latter group includes the rattlesnakes, the cottonmouth, and the copperhead.

The Coral Snakes The eastern coral snake is found from the Carolinas to central Texas. It is twenty to thirty-inches long and has bands of red, yellow, and black along its body. The key identifying feature of this snake is that the red and yellow rings touch each other. There are a number of harmless snakes that also have brightly colored bands, but in these species the red and yellow rings are separated by a black band and the red and yellow rings do not touch.

The eastern coral snake is a secretive creature. It is rarely seen in broad daylight. It preys on frogs, lizards, and other snakes. The venom of this snake is highly lethal and can be treated only with anti-venom and medical care.

There are a number of subspecies or races of the coral snake, such as the Texas coral snake and the Arizona coral snake. All of the coral snakes have a small mouth and short fangs. For this reason they cannot bite through clothing and sturdy footwear easily. However, naked toes and fingers are vulnerable.

The Pit Vipers The members of the pit viper family are characterized by deep facial pits on each side of the head, a little less than midway between the eye and the nostril. The mouths of these snakes have large, hollow fangs mounted on short maxillary bones. When the mouth is closed, the fangs are folded against the roof of the

◄*Motorists driving through big-game country should be vigilant. You never know when a deer may leap out in front of your car.*

mouth. The fangs rotate into an erect position only when the snake opens its mouth. The heads of most pit vipers are triangular in shape.

The *copperhead* is a fairly large snake, generally running between twenty-four and thirty-six inches in length. It has a coppery-red head with an hourglass pattern, hence its name. Its back and sides are covered with chestnut markings that are narrow at the top of the back and wide on the sides. Dark, rounded spots mark the belly.

There are several races of copperheads. The markings of these races vary slightly in detail and color.

Copperheads are found from Massachusetts south to Florida and from southern Illinois and Iowa to Texas. They live in a fairly wide range of habitats from rocky, wooded hillsides to low ground near swamps. Small rodents are their chief prey, but frogs are also eaten.

A great many snakes such as the milk snake, the fox snake, the hog snake, and the water snake are killed annually because they are mistaken for the copperhead. Although a fair number of people are bitten by copperheads, deaths are virtually nonexistent. The copperhead is not a serious threat to life.

The *cottonmouth* is a close relative of the copperhead. It is an even larger snake — thirty to forty-eight inches — and is almost entirely aquatic. It is olive brown or almost black in color when viewed from above. It has dark crossbands on its back and a light belly. The inside of the mouth is white, hence the name cottonmouth.

The cottonmouths are found from Virginia to Key West, west to Oklahoma and central Texas. The cottonmouth is basically an aquatic snake, living in swamps, lakes, rivers, and rice fields. It likes to sun itself on rocks and floating logs. On occasion, it may invade the uplands and be found hibernating with copperheads. Fish, frogs, salamanders, and even other snakes are the chief prey of the cottonmouth, but this snake is an opportunist and will eat anything that it can handle.

The cottonmouth is much more dangerous than the copperhead. It is a bigger snake, hence it is likely to inject more venom when it strikes. When excited, the cottonmouth will vibrate its tail. When fully aroused, it will throw its head backwards and open its jaws. The cottonmouth is aggressive. The splash of a paddle will frighten most other snakes away, but the cottonmouth is likely to stand its ground. Bass fishermen and hunters entering the southern swamps should learn to identify the cottonmouth at a glance. Again, many other water snakes are killed through ignorance because they are mistaken for the cottonmouth.

There are about a dozen species of *rattlesnakes* varying in size from fifteen to seventy-two inches. They range from New Hampshire, southern Ontario, and southern Saskatchewan southward right to the Gulf coast and into Mexico, and from New Jersey to California. As a group, the rattlesnakes live in a variety of habitats from rocky forests, to wet bottomlands and marshes, to deserts and grasslands. The hallmark of these snakes is, of course, the rattle on the tip of their tails. The rattle consists of loosely attached segments which strike against each other when the tail is vibrated. The rattle is best described as a buzzing noise, somewhat similar to that made by cicadas. The larger species produce the loudest noises. Generally rattlesnakes rattle only when angry or aroused — as a warning — but don't count on this. In cool weather the snake may be too lethargic to vibrate its tail. Certainly every outdoorsman should learn to recognize the rattle of a rattlesnake, as well as the snakes themselves.

The best way to learn to identify the rattlesnake — in fact, snakes of all kinds — is from exhibits of mounted specimens in museums or from live specimens in zoos and snake exhibits. Field guides to reptiles and amphibians are also useful.

By and large, the larger rattlesnakes — the diamondback and the timber rattlesnake — are more dangerous than the smaller species. Although all rattlesnakes, if given a chance, will try to escape, the larger ones are less apt to do so. When aroused, they will face the intruder and rattle vigorously. Unfortunately the diamondback and the timber rattlers live in country frequented by many fishermen, hikers, and campers.

There is no reason why anyone should ever be afraid of venturing out-of-doors into country where poisonous snakes are known to live. Snake bites are actually a very rare occurrence when compared to the host of other accidents that can befall an outdoorsman. We are many thousand times more likely to be killed driving to our favorite camping area or trout stream than we are to be bitten by a poisonous snake. Snake bites are rarely fatal; less than two people in every thousand that are bitten die.

Yet everyone traveling through country where poisonous snakes are known to be abundant should exhibit a bit of caution. Being observant is the first line of defense. Wearing good, sound, leather boots is another. The upland bird hunter can even obtain snake leggings made of aluminum mesh. If you are rockhounding or climbing in snake country, watch where you put your hands and what you grab. The same goes if you are picking berries or mushrooms. Use tools to overturn rocks and logs. Learn to recognize the buzzing rattle of a rattlesnake and even the billygoat odor that an aroused rattler sometimes emits.

I don't believe in killing any poisonous snake just because it is poisonous. In my opinion, the only time a man has the right to kill something is when he intends to eat it or when his life (and possibly his property) is being threatened or attacked. I have traveled through parts of the world where venomous snakes were abundant, and I have never been confronted or threatened by one. But if a rattlesnake suddenly crawled onto my back lawn and I had no way of disposing of it alive, I would kill it. This would also apply to a poisonous snake on a public campground where young children were playing.

TREATING A SNAKE BITE

There is a lot of controversy surrounding the treatment of snake bites. In the past, the recommended procedure was to apply a tourniquet, make an incision around the bite, and suck the fluids from the wound. This has generally been discredited by the medical profession because in many cases this treatment has been known to cause much harm. However, there are other things that can be done. Obviously the victim should be taken to a hospital as quickly as is feasible. If possible, the victim should be carried to a vehicle. If the victim has to move on his own, he should do so by walking slowly. The victim should be kept calm. No alcohol or other stimulants should be consumed by him. In short, everything possible should be done to keep his heartbeat normal.

If the bite is on the extremities, a tourniquet may help to keep the venom contained. Be sure not to have the tourniquet too tight and to loosen it every few minutes. You must not stop all circulation. Keep the bitten extremity lower to the ground than the heart. This will slow the movement of venom to the heart.

The use of ice as a cold pack in treating snake bite is also very controversial. It has been known to cause tissue damage and other problems. If ice has any beneficial role to play, it is only during the first hour or so after the bite.

Injections of anti-venom are the usual way of treating snake bite. Anti-venom, or AV as it is usually called, is a horse serum. Its misuse can be fatal. Generally it should be injected by a physician. It is available only on prescription. People who spend much time in country where poisonous snakes are abundant may wish to consult their family doctor about prescribing an AV kit so that they have it with them in case of emergency. AV is not always available in small hospitals. Many doctors may be reluctant to issue prescriptions because the AV kit comes with a syringe which has a needle about one-and-a-half inches long. It takes a fair amount of expertise to use such a needle. The needle is always injected into a thick muscle mass such as the buttocks or thigh. There is a further danger in the use of AV with people who cannot tolerate horse serum.

One thing is certain about snake bite. People in good physical condition are less apt to die or have serious problems than people who are soft and out of shape. Also, physically larger people tend to have an easier time. Children are more susceptible because they tend to panic and they are small.

OTHER REPTILES

There are two poisonous lizards in the world, and both are found in the southwest — the gila monster and the Mexican beaded lizard. Again, the bite of these lizards is seldom fatal. Indeed, people are seldom bitten by them. There are only little more than thirty recorded instances of bites to people. The Spanish explorer Francisco Hernandez recorded, back in 1577, that the bite was painful but not fatal.

There are a few other reptiles that one should be cautious of. The American alligator and American crocodile are two obvious ones, but they are seldom encountered in the wild except in the coastal regions of Louisiana and wilderness areas of Florida. Neither of these large reptiles has the dangerous reputation of some of the African species. The snapping turtle can inflict a painful bite, but does so only when someone annoys it on land. In water, the turtle makes every effort to get away. Some of the larger water snakes will bite if handled carelessly. The bites of these snakes are not poisonous, but in some cases they have been known to cause nausea.

The best precaution against wildlife hazards is to watch all wildlife with interest but at a safe distance. There is no reason why anyone should cause intentional stress to a wild creature by approaching it closely just to satisfy his idle curiosity.

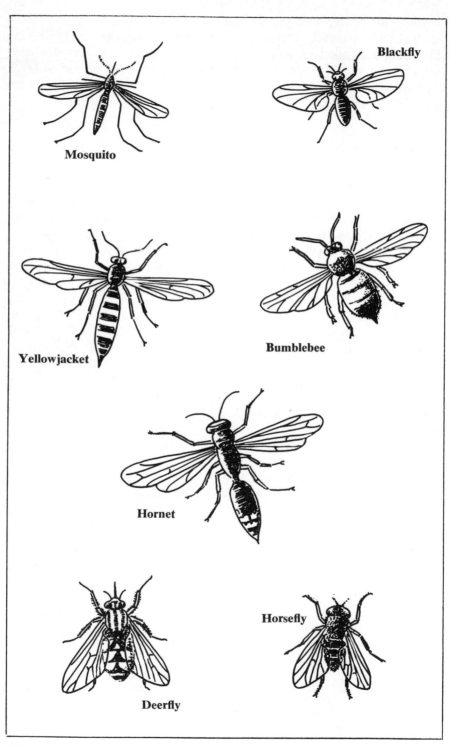

Mosquito

Blackfly

Yellowjacket

Bumblebee

Hornet

Deerfly

Horsefly

Chapter 4

Beating the Bugs

One of the biggest annoyances in the out-of-doors is biting and stinging insects. Indeed, some of these insect stings can be dangerous to hypersensitive individuals. But there are ways that biting insects can be beaten, or at least their bites kept to a minimum. Let's discuss the potentially dangerous insects first.

WASPS, HORNETS, AND BEES

Wasps, yellowjackets, bumblebees, and honeybees all carry venom that, on an equal volume basis, is as dangerous as the venom of a rattlesnake. Obviously these insects inject only minuscule doses of this poison at a time, but the venom is known to have an accumulative effect. The first few stings may bring on only normal symptoms of pain and slight swelling in the area of the injection. However, after several stings, the reaction may worsen and bring on a variety of serious symptoms including death. More people die annually in North America as a result of being stung by hornets, wasps, and other stinging insects than as a result of snake bites.

Precautionary measures are the first defense. Don't disturb these insects or their nests. Wear neutral-colored clothing such as off-whites, tans, and greens; bright colors attract them, and bees actually seem to be angered by black. Don't use sweet or strong-smelling perfumes and after-shave lotions. These also appear to attract bees, wasps, and hornets. Keep food, particularly sweet things, covered at all times. After your meal, don't leave such food on picnic tables.

◄*Biting insects are always annoying. The mosquito, the blackfly, the horsefly, and the deerfly are just that. But the yellowjacket, the hornet, and even the honeybee can be hazardous.*

Put it away in your tent or cooler. Don't put wildflowers on picnic tables. Wear shoes; yellowjackets live in the ground.

Bee stings, surprisingly enough, cause more deaths than wasps, yellowjackets, and hornets combined. The reason no doubt is due to their great numbers. Most people are stung by bees at home in their own garden or back yard, rather than in the wilds.

Wasps, hornets and yellowjackets are dangerous because frequently they attack in swarms. A single wasp nest may hold 10,000 insects. For some reason youngsters like to throw rocks and sticks at such nests. This is one sure way of inviting trouble. Bumblebees rarely sting.

What should you do if you get stung? Well, there are several things you can do. If you have been stung by a bee, the stinger will still be in the wound. A bee can sting only once because its stinger has barbs that embed it in the wound. The bee will tear the stinger from its body when it flies off, and it will die moments later. So first you must remove the stinger from the wound as fast as you can. The longer the stinger remains, the more venom the poison sac will release into the wound through its hollow needle. Don't pick the stinger off, because by grasping the top end where the poison sac is, you will inject more venom into the wound. Instead, scrape it off with a knife blade, a wooden match, or even a fingernail. Now, as fast as you can, apply ice from your ice chest to the wound. This will slow down the spreading of the poison. Keep away from heat. Mud applications have been recommended for stings in the past, but forget it unless the mud is ice cold. Ammonia is equally useless.

Hornet and wasp stings will not leave a stinger in the wound. These insects can inflict more than one sting at a time. The treatment is the same as for bee stings except, of course, there is no stinger to remove. Medical attention should be sought immediately if multiple stings have been received or if hypersensitivity to such stings is suspected or known.

Anyone who suffers badly from asthma or hayfever or has a strong reaction when stung by common insects such as mosquitos, horseflies, and deerflies, should treat wasp, hornet and bee stings with extreme caution.

There are special first-aid kits on the market for people who are hypersensitive to the stings of bees, wasps, hornets, and the like. Generally these are available only with a doctor's prescription. If you or one of your family is hypersensitive, you should consult your family doctor about having this type of kit with you at home and on outdoor rambles.

These kits contain pills, sterile alcohol pads, a tourniquet, and a hypodermic syringe with 0.3 ml of Epinephrine, plus an instruction folder. The medication in the syringe serves to slow down the poison's reaction until the pills begin to work.

SCORPIONS AND SPIDERS

The black widow spider and the scorpion are two other insects that an outdoorsman may, on rare occasions, encounter. Bites from both of these insects are dangerous, but only rarely lethal.

Generally black widow spiders are found in rubbish heaps and old ramshackle buildings. If you are fond of visiting old ghost towns, abandoned mines, and other similar spots, you should exercise a bit of caution.

Scorpions are nocturnal insects. They spend their days under rocks, brush piles, and leaves. The only real hazard is that they may choose some shaded spot in camp, such as a rubber mattress, under which to hide as dawn approaches. If you are traveling in scorpion country, it is wise to exhibit a bit of caution by shaking out your boots and checking over your sleeping bag before using them.

A bite from a scorpion or a black widow may cause swelling, pain, nausea, fever, and even speech and breathing difficulties. Obviously the more allergic the person is to these venoms, the more drastic is the reaction. Children are more susceptible than adults, but as I said earlier, death due to black widow or scorpion bites occurs rarely and then only in extreme cases. Anyone bitten by these insects should be taken to a doctor immediately. First aid should consist of an application of an ice pack, ice water, or simply a chunk of ice to the bitten area. If the bite is on a foot or a hand, a tourniquet can be used. The tourniquet must be applied with extreme care. Never tie the tourniquet too tightly and be sure to release it every few minutes. The bitten person should be kept calm. The heart beat and pulse of an excited person are much faster than normal, hence the venom spreads much more quickly. The bitten person should not walk more than necessary. Remember, exercise also quickens heart beat and pulse.

MOSQUITOS AND BLACKFLIES

Mosquitos and blackflies are two of the most common pests that an outdoorsman has to endure. Usually they are worse during early to mid-spring but, in some areas such as the Arctic, they can be troublesome during the entire summer.

Fortunately both of these insects are easy to combat. Proper clothing is the first and best line of defense. Clothes should be loose on the body and of fairly tightly woven material. With such clothes, the mosquito's mouth parts cannot penetrate to the bare skin. Clothing should be light in color; off-whites and light khakis are much less attractive to blackflies and mosquitos than darker colors. Blackflies in particular are attracted to dark colors. In very bad blackfly country, the pantlegs and cuffs of shirt sleeves should be tied around the ankle and wrist or, in the case of pantlegs, tucked into boots, so that the insects cannot get inside clothing.

Insect repellents are the second and excellent form of defense. There are a vast number of these on the market, but the best by far that I have ever tested is Cutter's. Most insect repellents can be obtained in aerosol sprays, oils, jellies, and sticks. They all have their advantages and disadvantages. Aerosol sprays are good because they can be sprayed over clothing. Oils and jellies stay on the skin much longer, giving better protection and they are less easily washed off by sweat.

In areas where mosquitos and blackflies are very troublesome, a mosquito head net and even a pair of cotton gloves are good means of protection. These are particularly good if you are doing something like wildlife photography where you cannot move about or swat at insects without alarming your subjects. Then dark gloves and a head net also serve as camouflage for your white face and hands.

Smoke, both from a fire and a pipe, is a good defensive or offensive weapon against both blackflies and mosquitos. Smoke is just about the only thing the Indians had, and don't think that Indians weren't troubled by these bugs. They were and are, but they also had a philosophical attitude that these insects were unavoidable and they had to put up with them. Clouds of blackflies did not excite them — frighten them — as much as they do some white men. However, I have observed that many of the younger Indians in the northern bush are reacting to mosquitos and blackflies as badly as some white men. Our race is not the only one whose children have gone soft.

Another good defense against blackflies and mosquitos is wind. When walking, stick to high ridges, open fields, and lake shores where the wind is stronger. Make your campsite on breezy islands, open ridges, and points. Your tent should have a good fly screen and a sewn-in floor.

Blackflies breed in running water. That is why they are more troublesome in the spring when the run-off is strong. Once the upland rills have dried up, blackflies decline in numbers very sharply. If you are out during blackfly season, it is a good idea to make your camp away from running water — away from the fly source. On the other hand, mosquitos breed in stagnant water. Once such pools and ponds dry up, mosquitos also decline in number. Again, you can minimize the effect of these insects by making camp as far away as possible from their breeding habitat. With mosquitos, it is the female that causes the problem. The male is strictly a vegetarian; the female needs a blood meal — protein — for the development of eggs.

HORSEFLIES AND DEERFLIES

Deerflies and horseflies are two very aggressive insects. They will follow and attack incessantly. Loose, tightly woven clothing is the best defense. Insect repellents help, but they are not as effective against mosquitos and blackflies. A head net is very effective where these two insects are most troublesome, but generally the peak deerfly and horsefly season is in the summer when hot weather makes a head net even more uncomfortable than deerfly or horsefly bites.

Both of these insects are most common in areas where cattle and horses are abundant or in good big-game country. The more deer, elk, or moose in an area, the more deerflies and horseflies. If you are rambling about in big-game country hoping to see, photograph, or bag a deer, elk, or moose, you will have to put up with these flies during the summer and early fall.

CHIGGERS AND ITCH MITES

Chiggers are almost microscopic. One of these little red devils is about 1/200 (.005) of an inch long. They live on vegetation — brush and tall grass — and are picked up on your clothing as you walk by. Once they hitch a ride on a human, they crawl into the warm areas — under the armpits, under the wristwatch strap, and into the groin.

The itch mite is about the same size as the chigger and is white or pale yellow in color. The female burrows under the skin and lays eggs. As it burrows, it feeds on the tissue and releases a toxin that dissolves tissues and causes swelling and itching.

If you are traveling in chigger and itch mite country, keep away from stands of thick, lush vegetation whenever possible. Keeping pantlegs inside boots may also help. Dusting ankles, wrists, necklines, and other exposed areas with powdered sulphur is a good bet if chiggers or itch mites are really bad. In the evenings, if at all possible, take hot, soapy baths or a shower. Water will wash chiggers and itch mites off. There are also ointments on the market that kill both of these insects. Drugstores in chigger and itch mite country generally stock these ointments.

TICKS

Ticks are very common insect pests. They live by sucking blood. They can also transmit a disease known as spotted fever, but this disease is not at all prevalent. Most ticks are brown or green in color and are about one-quarter of an inch long — before they gorge themselves with blood. Blood-filled ticks may be several times the length of ticks that have not fed.

Ticks are picked up off vegetation and, like chiggers, they crawl to some area of bare skin. Here they bite painlessly through the skin and bury their heads in. A favorite area for ticks on humans is the back of the neck along the hairline or the back of the ears. When traveling in known tick country, check your clothing carefully and your body every night. Insect repellent sprayed on clothing acts as a deterrent to some extent.

Exercise great care when removing ticks to insure that you do not simply tear off the body and leave the insect's head or mouth parts under the skin where they may fester. Ticks may be removed with tweezers in one hand and a pin or needle in the other. The pin or needle is used to pry the mouth loose. A slower and safer way to remove ticks is to coat the insect heavily with a greasy lotion — vaseline or molten paraffin. These materials shut off the air supply from the insect and eventually force it to let go. Burning the insect with a cigarette is also effective and it can then be picked off with tweezers. Dabbing the insect with rubbing alcohol will generally also make it let go.

One last tip about ticks. Dogs are very susceptible to them. If you are out with your dog in tick country, examine the animal very carefully every evening.

CATERPILLARS

There are a number of caterpillars — the puss caterpillar, the hag-moth caterpillar, and the saddleback caterpillar — that have irritating secretions in their hairs. These secretions can cause itching and nasty, painful blisters. If you cannot recognize the different species of caterpillars, don't touch any of them — just look.

COPING WITH ITCHING BITES

The bites of blackflies, sandflies, mosquitos, itch mites, and chiggers all itch. The severity of the itching depends on the sensitivity of the individual bitten and, of course, on the extent of the bites. Swelling is usual, particularly from mosquito and itch mite bites. Scratching the bites can cause a secondary infection to develop and it, of course, makes the itching worse.

Use ice to alleviate the swelling. A mixture of baking soda and water in a thick paste will help to alleviate itching. Calamine lotion is helpful and should be included among items to take when venturing into bug country. The commercial preparation Absorbine Jr. is also good for treating mosquito bites that itch and have swollen.

POISON IVY

Chapter 5

Poisonous Plants

There are a number of members of the plant world that are poisonous to man in one form or another. The chapter on wilderness survival delves a little into plants that are poisonous to eat. This chapter deals with plants that most commonly produce an adverse reaction when touched — poison ivy, poison sumac, and poison oak. At one time or another most outdoorsmen come across one or all of these plants. However, some people react to them much more severely than others. Some people don't react at all.

All of these plants produce toxic chemical agents that can cause anything from mild itching to severe blistering when they come in contact with skin. For sensitive people, only a small amount of the toxic material is needed to produce a severe reaction. Most commonly people come in contact with the toxins of these plants by walking through a patch or rubbing against poisonous climbing plants on trees and fences. However, there are other ways in which the toxin can be transferred. Often dogs pick up the toxin on their coats and transfer it to persons who touch them. Insects pick up the poison on their feet and then land on exposed hands or arms. Hikers pick it up on their boots and pantlegs and then touch it with bare hands when removing their clothing.

The chemical that causes all the misery is a phenol found in the sap of the plant. This is why it is much more prevalent during the spring and early summer (the growing season) than during the fall or winter.

The best method of dealing with poison ivy, poison sumac, and poison oak is to learn to recognize the plants and to avoid contact with them.

POISON IVY

Poison ivy is by far the most common troublemaker. Commonly

it grows in thickets, open woods, sandy or rocky places, and on fence rows through most of the United States except in some very arid regions. It is fairly abundant in southern Quebec, Ontario, the Great Lakes region, and the mid-west. It is not known to grow above the tree line.

Poison ivy is a twining, climbing vine that is almost shrub-like in appearance, but it can also support itself by aerial roots on the trunks of trees and on fences, or it can be found in partially shaded wood-lots among low growing plants such as ferns.

Poison ivy has one easily recognizable characteristic — its compound leaf consisting of three leaflets. These leaflets are a bright, glossy green, oval-shaped, and smoothly textured. They are clustered together and have sharply tipped points and widely serrated edges.

The flowers of poison ivy, present in the spring and early summer, are borne in clusters and are small and inconspicuous. The flowers are dainty, and vary in color from greenish white to cream. Close-knit clusters of berries, also greenish white or cream, develop from these flowers, and become hard and waxy when mature. These berries persist through the winter and are a favorite and harmless food for many species of birds. Not all poison ivy plants have berries.

Such plants as poison ivy, poison oak, and poison sumac have toxic oils which can cause symptoms ranging from mild itching to severe skin blisters. Learn to recognize these plants.

POISON SUMAC

POISON SUMAC

Poison sumac is a coarse shrub or a small tree generally ranging from four to twenty feet in height. It also has compound leaves, but the number of leaflets ranges from seven to thirteen. These leaflets occur opposite each other on the branch, and have one terminal leaflet at the end of the branch. Poison sumac prefers wet, boggy, acid soils and thus generally occurs in wooded swamps. Its range extends through most of the south and southeastern United States, along the east coast into New England, through New York, the Great Lakes, and the mid-western states, and through southwestern Quebec and southern Ontario.

Poison sumac flowers are similar to those of poison ivy, but they grow in hanging clusters and originate in the axils of leaves. Poison sumac fruits are shiny, ivory-colored berries that hang in loose and droopy bunches. These bunches may be as long as a foot. The berries persist throughout winter and provide food for many bird species.

POISON OAK

Poison oak is quite similar to poison ivy in appearance, but its leaves are thicker and smaller in size, and the ends of the leaves are rounded rather than pointed. Generally poison oak has the same triple-leaflet formation, but occasionally five leaflets are produced. The outline of the poison oak leaflet somewhat resembles the leaf of the white oak, hence its name.

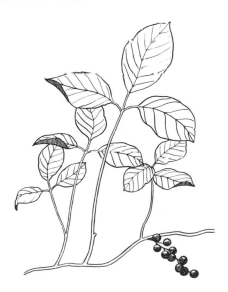

POISON OAK

Poison oak prefers dry barrens, pine lands, and sands, and is most prevalent in the coastal regions. Along the Atlantic coast it favors poor sandy soils and flourishes in the company of scrub oak and pine. Poison oak was one of the plants most feared by the Cherokee Indians.

Poisoning from any of these plants may result any time after contact, from a few hours to a few days. The most common signs of contamination are itching and inflammation of the skin, followed by the emergence of watery blisters. However, the poison will not spread from a broken blister — the persistent development of new patches of itching and inflammation means that the toxin is being spread from contaminated clothing or from contact with more plants.

The effects of these poisonous plants are very severe on some persons, sometimes requiring hospitalization. If you suspect that you have been in contact with any of these plants, the best procedure is to lather copiously with a good, strong, yellow laundry soap, rinse thoroughly, and then repeat the procedure again. If, after this, itching and inflammation still develop, the wisest procedure is to visit a family physician. A one-percent solution of potassium permanganate swabbed over the infected area is known to give some relief from the itching. The brown stains produced from this material can be removed with lemon juice. Certain iron salts have also been used for the relief of itching, particularly ferric chloride. This material is mixed with a quarter glycerin, a quarter alcohol, and half water, and is swabbed on the affected spots, but it stains as well. Calamine lotion sometimes affords relief from minor itching.

STINGING NETTLE

There are a few other plants besides the above that can be troublesome to the outdoorsman. Among them are the stinging or spurge nettles. The stinging nettle is the more common of the two. The stinging nettle is a bushy looking plant with leaves that are very coarsely toothed and stiff bristles that "sting" on contact. The plants run from six to thirty inches in height, and are found in waste places, sand hills, road sides, and so on from Newfoundland west to Manitoba, and through portions of the mid-western United States east to northeastern Virginia. Again, the best way of dealing with stinging nettle is to learn to recognize and avoid it.

Chapter 6

Map and Compass

No one should venture into the wilderness without a compass, not even if his only intention is to go over the ridge to pick blueberries. Most outdoor recreationists today are urban dwellers. Often their knowledge about the country into which they are venturing is skimpy. Many campers and fishermen set off on trips into the wilderness or go for a walk from their camp without really knowing how to read landmarks. Many don't even carry a compass and, of those who do, many don't know how to use it. It is no surprise to me that newspapers and newscasts regularly carry reports of lost hikers, campers, and hunters.

Knowing how to use a compass is a must for anyone who calls himself an outdoorsman. It is one of the primary outdoor skills, like using an ax. Experienced woodsmen, trappers, and such rarely rely on a compass to find their way. But generally they have an uncanny sense of direction. This sense is based on many things, including the lay of the land and the ability to see and absorb inconspicuous landmarks and it comes as a result of many years in the bush.

Most of us are not that fortunate. For example, it is difficult to completely lose a sense of direction on a sunny day. But an overcast day is something else. With no sun to guide us, we can get mixed up very easily. A compass will give the right direction every time.

A compass is a simple device. It is a steel needle, magnetized so that one end will always point to the earth's magnetic pole which lies a thousand miles south of the true North Pole and a little west of the hundred-degree meridian. Some compasses use a magnetized disc rather than a needle.

CHOOSING A COMPASS

Although compasses can be used for navigation and survey work,

the outdoorsman's basic interest lies in keeping on a straight course to some distant point and then coming back again. For this, a small hand-held compass with a swing needle or a disc is adequate. Such compasses come in many styles. The more sophisticated ones have needles that float in oil to dampen their swinging and have sights for taking headings. Others have levers which allow the needle to be taken off the pivot when the compass is not being used. I think that the very simple compasses are not wise choices for the serious outdoorsman. They are frequently chosen because they are small and inexpensive. A good compass, such as the Sylva and others in its class, can be used for fairly sophisticated work. These are sturdy and dependable. For approximately $15 to $20, they are a good life insurance policy.

All magnetic compasses react to iron and steel, and other magnets, including other compasses. If you are carrying something made of iron — a rifle, a knife, or a belt buckle — it can throw the needle off. A simple test can be conducted to check for this. Simply place the compass on a low stump and walk away a few steps, giving the needle time to come to a full stop. As you turn, watch the needle to see if it swings towards you as you approach. If it does, you must find out what is causing the needle to deviate and get rid of it whenever you take a compass reading.

USING MAP AND COMPASS

Since the compass needle points to the magnetic pole, you must compensate for the difference between the positions of the true North Pole and the magnetic north. This difference is called declination and it varies from nearly zero degrees to twenty-five degrees east or west depending on what part of the continent the reading is being taken from. The near zero degrees applies if the reading is taken when the magnetic north and the true north are in line. However, the only time declination is of concern is when you are trying to follow a map that has both magnetic-variance lines and grid lines based on the true north. Declination needs to be known for navigation. Both Geodetic Survey and U.S. Coast maps show magnetic variance as dotted lines and grid lines as solid lines. Declination is always given in degrees east and west. But more about this later.

The elementary way of using a compass is as a direction finder.

◄*No one should venture into a wilderness area without a map, a good compass, and a knowledge of how to use both.*

To do this, you must simply wait until the needle stops, turn the dial until the north arrow and the needle are aligned, and then use whatever bearing will bring you to your destination. In such elementary compassing, declination is ignored. However, this technique works well only when short distances are involved or when the objective is large such as a road or a river and you don't care where you hit it. A variation of this technique can also be used to reach an objective that is visible only at times. In this case you simply take a compass heading and use it whenever you lose sight of the objective.

However, for more sophisticated compassing such as hitting a bay on a small lake many miles away, a map is needed on which the location of the camp is pinpointed. The technique here depends on the type of compass.

Determining a course with a simple compass:

1. Draw a line from your starting point to the objective.

2. If the map has no north-south line running across your intended line of travel, then draw one by joining two points of the same longitude.

3. Place a protractor along the north-south line with the center point at the junction of your path of travel and the north-south line.

4. Read the bearing of the path of travel in degrees at the outer margin of the protractor. Let us say that it is eighty degrees.

5. Now you must convert the map's true north bearing to a magnetic north bearing by applying the declination shown on the map. Let us assume that the declination is ten degrees E. Then the bearing you have to follow to reach your objective is seventy degrees E — the declination (ten degrees E) minus the reading of your path of travel as shown by the protractor (eighty degrees).

Determining a course with a Sylva
or other good quality compass:

1. Place your map on a flat, level surface. If you wish, you can draw a line from the objective to the starting point, but this is not necessary.

2. Align the transparent plate of your compass along the path of travel so that the line of sight is pointing in that direction.

3. Turn the compass until the lines on the housing are parallel to the north-south lines on the map. If the map does not have north-south lines, you will have to draw one crossing your path of travel. The north arrow on the housing will now be pointing to true north.

4. Turn the compass housing the number of degrees of declination marked on the map. (If the declination is east, this means a clockwise turn; if the declination is west, an anti-clockwise turn.) The index pointer now reads the magnetic bearing of the path of travel.

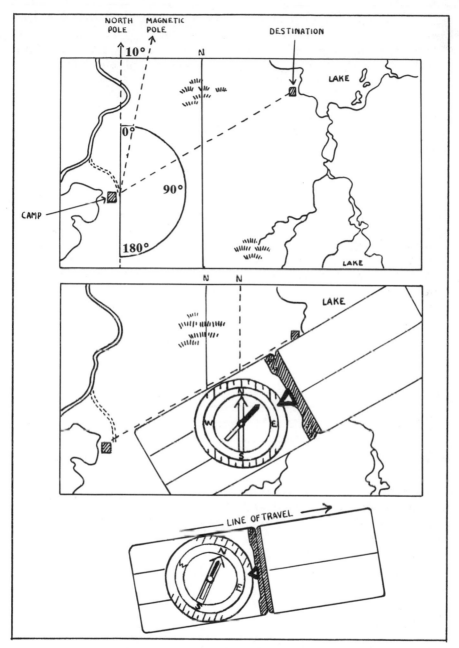

Determining a course of travel with a simple compass is easy. Draw a line from your starting point to the objective. Place a protractor on the north-south line of your map. Read the bearing of the path of travel in degrees. Then convert the map's true north to magnetic north by applying the declination.

5. To travel the line of direction required, turn the whole compass without moving the housing so that the north end of the needle points over the north end of the engraved arrow. The course to travel will be the line of sight or the direction of the sides of the transparent plate.

Occasionally someone gets lost in spite of having a compass and knowing how to use it, usually because the traveler lacked confidence in the compass. He "knew" that the compass was wrong and that his sense of direction was right. Compasses seldom lie. They may be affected by something outside the magnetic influence, but that's up to the compass-man to discover ahead of time. The compass-man may also make mistakes. If he reads the headings incorrectly, he cannot blame the compass for getting him lost.

Learning how to use a compass can be great fun. The way to start is in territory that you know. If you can follow bearings with good accuracy in familiar country, you are ready for the wilderness.

No one should go into an unfamiliar wilderness area without a good map. For canoe tripping, a map with a scale of two miles to one inch is fine. For hiking, a map with a larger scale is better, preferably one with contour lines. Familiarize yourself with the map first. Look at the topographical features that you will encounter along your route or path of travel. Learn the legend. To protect your map from moisture, cover it with clear, self-adhesive plastic sheeting or spray it with a clear plastic spray. There are also plastic map cases available which allow the map to be folded so that the sections that are in use are visible. These are a good idea on any trip.

WILDERNESS MAPS

Topographical maps can be a tremendous asset to any outdoorsman. A topo map is different from a road map because it shows the features of the land — the topography. Also, it shows the type of vegetation, old logging roads, foot trails, cabins, mining and lumber camps, power lines, streams, swamps, and springs. By studying a topo map, an outdoorsman can get a good picture of what an area looks like and what he can expect to find there.

Of all the millions of words that have been written giving advice to outdoorsmen on virtually every form of outdoor recreation, surprisingly little has been said about the usefulness of topographical maps. I would no more dream of going on a wilderness trip of any sort — fishing, hunting, backpacking, canoeing, ski touring, or snowmobiling — without a topographical map of the area, than I would of going without an ax. The topographical map will not only show me landmarks, help me with navigation, and tell me what kind of terrain lies ahead, but it will give me an idea of the type of wild-life and fish habitats I might encounter. Marshes may hold water-fowl. Small, spring-fed mountain streams and ponds may have trout. The marshy lakes of northern Canada are ideal places to look for moose during summer and early fall because moose like to feed on aquatic vegetation. The list of possibilities is endless.

Even in settled farm country, topographical maps are of immense value. I have used them to locate tiny hidden trout streams, small marshes where other waterfowlers are seldom encountered, likely looking woodcock covers along streams, and moist swales, and high hardwood ridges with interesting snowshoeing and ski touring possi-bilities. By using the topo maps first and scouting the area, I am able to get away from the hordes of other outdoorsmen by finding little pockets of woodlands tucked away out of sight from roads.

The key to using a topographical map lies in learning the symbols and codes. They tell the story of what actually lies on the ground. Generally the maps cover one quadrangle, one-quarter degree of latitude and longitude. The scale of the map can vary, but the larger the scale, the more detail the map shows and the more valuable it is. The most useful scale is a seven-and-a-half-minute quadrangle series. On this scale, one inch on the map represents about two thousand feet on the ground.

Topographical maps in the United States can be obtained from the Map Information Office, U.S. Geological Survey, Washington, D.C. 20244, for states east of the Mississippi. Maps of states west of the Mississippi can be obtained from the Map Information Office, U.S. Geological Survey, Federal Center, Denver, Colorado 80225. In Canada, topo maps can be obtained from the Map Distribution Office, Department of Mines and Technical Service, Ottawa, Ontario.

First you will need an index sheet for the state or province you are interested in, telling what maps are available. With this index, you will get instructions as to how to order individual maps. You can then select the maps for the area you want and order them. Topo-graphical maps are quite inexpensive.

Topographical maps for national parks can be purchased over-the-counter at all park headquarters. It is also possible to purchase topographical maps of national forests in the United States at the U.S. Forest Service Regional Center in Atlanta, Georgia; Milwaukee, Wisconsin; Albuquerque, New Mexico; Denver, Colorado; Ogden, Utah; Missoula, Montana; San Francisco, California; Portland, Ore-gon; and Juneau, Alaska.

One last tip. When maps are requested by mail, you should allow about four weeks for delivery, so plan your trip early and order your maps well ahead of time.

Rubber Eyecup (folded to show use by person with eyeglasses)

Rubber Eyecup (extended to show use by person with normal vision)

Exit pupil (Rear Lens)

Focusing Wheel

Bridge

Correction Wheel for Right Eyepiece

Objective Lens

Binoculars are the most useful piece of equipment an outdoorsman can own. They have an all-season use and bring year-round pleasure.

60

Chapter 7

Optics for the Outdoorsman

If someone were to ask me what piece of outdoor equipment gives me the greatest pleasure, I would have no difficulty in answering — binoculars. Aside from my knives, binoculars are the only piece of equipment I use year around. Canoes, tents, snowshoes, fishing rods, shotguns, and rifles all have seasonal uses, but not binoculars. I generally carry a pair of binoculars, or at least have a pair handy, on almost every outdoor ramble.

When the fishing has hit the doldrums, binoculars have never failed to provide me with entertainment. I have watched ospreys fishing, beavers repairing their dams, and minks hunting for a meal along a lakeshore. In the blue bird days of fall, I have pleasantly idled away many hours in a duck blind watching marsh birds and other creatures. And more than a little of my reputation as a big-game hunter is the result of using binoculars. On a big-game hunt, I consider binoculars to be much more beneficial than the 'scope on my rifle. As a bird watcher and a wildlife photographer, I have found them to be indispensable.

Curiously enough, binoculars do not actually extend your range of vision beyond what you can see with the naked eye. In other words, they don't help you see farther. What they do is make distant objects look more detailed, larger, and clearer. They do this not only by magnifying, but also by gathering and transmitting light through the lenses and prisms to the eye.

BINOCULAR SAVVY

Magnification The magnification is one of the principal considerations in selecting binoculars. There is a tendency among inexperienced outdoorsmen to select binoculars with high magnification. The theory is that if it is higher in power, it has to be better.

61

This is wrong. Binoculars of high power are difficult to hold steady; the tremors of your hand are magnified in proportion to the magnification of the binoculars.

Binoculars of a moderate power — 7X or 8X — are the best all-around choice. Although binoculars can be had with 16X or 20X magnification, these require tripods for satisfactory use. About the highest practical magnification for an outdoorsman is 10X.

Brightness   The relative brightness or the "ability to gather light" is another important feature to consider in binoculars. Although magnification plays a part in this, a bigger role is played by the diameter of the objective lens. Generally speaking, the wider the objective lens, the greater the relative brightness. However, magnification can negate the relative brightness. For example, binoculars of the specifications 10X50 and 7X50 have the same diameter-objective lens, but the 7X50 have higher relative brightness. Binoculars with very wide objective lenses are generally bulky and heavy and should not be selected where compactness and weight are important factors.

Field of View   The field of view is the width or diameter of the circular view that you see through the binoculars. It is always measured at a thousand yards. A wider field of view allows the viewer to take in more territory without moving the glasses. A wide field of view is an asset, particularly when viewing fast moving objects at close range. Again, the higher the magnification, the lower the field of view. There are binoculars on the market with extra-wide fields of view. These sell at higher prices than the same binoculars with standard fields of view.

Focusing   There are two different focusing systems in binoculars — central focusing and individual focusing. In binoculars with individual focusing, each eyepiece is focused individually according to a calibrated scale on it. With central focusing, both eyepieces are focused simultaneously by turning a knurled knob between the barrels. On most such binoculars, the right eyepiece has a scale for adjusting the visual difference between your two eyes. Very few people have the same vision in both eyes.

The advantage of centrally focused binoculars is the ease and convenience of focusing. Most high quality binoculars manufactured today have central focusing. Individual-focus binoculars are fine if only one person is using them because the focus will not be changed. They are somewhat simpler in construction, hence they are less expensive.

Coating   On high quality binoculars, the lenses are always coated with magnesium fluoride on the air-to-glass surface. This coating eliminates reflections and glare and allows greater light transmission.

Reflected light bounces off the prisms in the binoculars, reaching the eye as haze and making the image less sharp.

Alignment The barrels of binoculars must be in perfect alignment, or your eyes won't be able to make one image out of two. You can safely assume that any new pair of binoculars, when purchased, will be in perfect alignment. However, with cheap and flimsy binoculars, the alignment can change with use. When a change in alignment is only slight, your eyes can compensate for it, but using non-aligned binoculars will cause you eyestrain and headaches. The best protection against non-alignment lies in the reputation of the manufacturer and his guarantee. All high quality binoculars are sold with a guarantee of anywhere from five years to a lifetime.

Definition The definition — the clarity and sharpness — of binoculars changes from the center to the edge of the viewing field. No binoculars have perfect center-to-edge definition. However, in binoculars with good optics, the edge definition has deteriorated to such a low point that it is almost unnoticeable. When purchasing binoculars, compare the edge definition in binoculars of different price brackets by focusing on a flat surface such as a wall.

Coloring High quality binoculars are always corrected for colors most noticeable to the eyes. Look through binoculars at a dark object against a bright sky to see if you get rainbows or strong color fringes. These color fringes impair good definition.

Other Features When purchasing good binoculars examine their general appearance. Make sure that the binoculars are well finished. See that the focusing mechanism and the hinges work smoothly. Look at the external covering on the barrels to ascertain that it is attached well. If you can afford only low-priced binoculars, shake them to see if any screws or prisms are loose inside. Look at the external parts to see how well they are cemented together. Give the objective lens a tap with your knuckle to make sure that it is mounted solidly. Read the manufacturer's guarantee and compare it with the guarantees of competitive brands.

SELECTING BINOCULARS

Buying binoculars can be a baffling business. There are a great many models to choose from and in many price ranges. Binoculars with seemingly similar features can vary as much as two hundred dollars in price. And then there is the question of magnification and the diameter of the objective lens. Almost everyone knows that binoculars designated as 7X35 or 10X50 means that the binoculars rated as 7X will magnify seven times, while those rated at 10X will magnify ten times. The figures thirty-five and fifty are the diameters of the objective lenses in millimeters.

The best all-around binoculars for the outdoors are 7X35. Such a glass is easy to hold without undue hand tremor. It has good light-gathering abilities for forest use on dark days. It is an excellent choice for bird watching, hunting, and even for spectator sports.

Another good choice is 8X30. It offers a bit more magnification, but less light-gathering ability. It is suitable for big-game hunting and bird watching. Another popular glass is 9X35. This is a binocular for open country — mountains and plains. It is not as easy to hold steady as a 7X35 and is best used when the viewer can sit down and brace his elbows against his upright knees to steady his hands.

Binoculars such as 10X50 are for long-range viewing, but they are too bulky and heavy if you have other gear to carry as well. For night use and for navigation, 7X50 are the best bet. These binoculars are also bulky and heavy, but they have tremendous light-gathering ability.

On the other hand, binoculars such as 6X25 are a little too small for general use. However, because of their small size and lightness

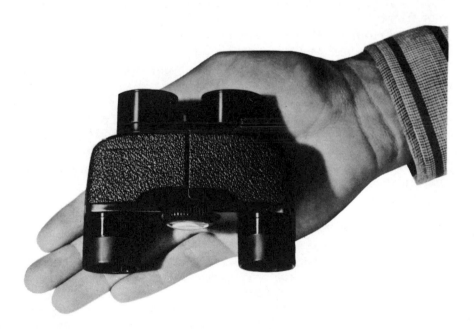

Binoculars come in various powers and sizes ranging from the big 10x50 to the compact 6x25 which can easily be shoved into a jacket pocket.

they can be shoved into the pocket of a jacket and taken along when bulkier and heavier binoculars would be left behind. This is why I own such a pair.

Most high quality binoculars today are made in the United States, West Germany, and Japan. The only American manufacturer is Bausch and Lomb. Their binoculars are expensive, but of outstanding quality. The 9X35 Bausch and Lomb binoculars are the choice of many knowledgeable mountain hunters. One can hardly go wrong in choosing binoculars by Bausch and Lomb.

Three outstanding German makes are Zeiss, Leitz, and Hensoldt. Zeiss lenses are world renowned and their binoculars are excellent. Zeiss makes a very fine 8X30 binocular crated entirely in rubber for maximum water resistance and protection against non-alignment if the binoculars are accidentally dropped. The rubber absorbs most of the shock.

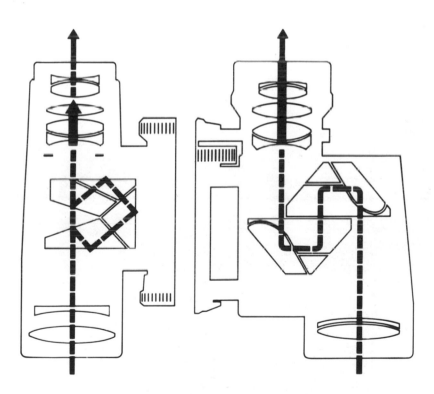

The two basic types of binoculars are the roof prismatic (left) and the Potro prism (right). The roof prismatic binoculars have the advantage of being only half the weight and one-quarter less bulky than the conventional Potro prism binoculars.

Leitz, the manufacturers of Leica cameras, make several models of roof-prismatic binoculars. These Leitz Trinovid binoculars have their prisms arranged in a different way which makes them very slim and light. Indeed, Leitz binoculars are one-third to one-half lighter and one-quarter to one-third less bulky than binoculars with comparable magnification and objective lenses of the conventional Potroprism design. The Trinovids are made in 7X35, 8X32, and 10X40. The 10X40's are smaller and lighter than conventional 7X35's. The only hangup with these Leitz binoculars is their price — over four hundred dollars for the 10X40's. The other powers are a little less expensive.

Excellent binoculars are made in Japan. Indeed, the Japanese have captured most of the low and medium-priced binocular market. Such camera manufacturers as Pentax and Nikon both make good, medium-priced binoculars. But perhaps the best known brand is Bushnell.

A serious birdwatcher or big-game hunter in the mountains may also find a spotting 'scope very useful. Spotting 'scopes have magnification ranges from 20 to 30 power.

Bushnell glasses are excellent, and are made in many styles ranging from low to medium in price. I have used Bushnell binoculars in 7X35 and 6X25 with great satisfaction. Other Japanese manufacturers are Tasco and Swift. Low-priced Japanese-made binoculars can be had for fifty dollars, while the medium-priced binoculars range from about one hundred to one hundred and fifty dollars.

OTHER OPTICS

Some outdoorsmen may find other optical instruments useful. For example, the rock hound and the botany bug may need a magnifying lens for evaluation and identification of specimens. A serious bird watcher and a big-game hunter in the mountains may want a spotting 'scope. These are powerful instruments with magnifications ranging from 20X to 30X.

The criteria for selecting spotting 'scopes are essentially the same as for selecting binoculars. Spotting 'scopes cannot be hand-held for viewing efficiency. They must be mounted on a tripod which will elevate them to a standing position or to a prone position. Bird watchers will prefer a tall tripod such as one used in photography. Big-game hunters generally prefer a prone tripod because it is shorter and lighter and because hunters prefer to remain hidden and inconspicuous as they peer over mountain ledges.

Chapter 8

The Outdoorsman's Knife

The knife is one of man's earliest tools. Its history goes back to the stirrings of time when our ancient ancestors first used a sharp piece of stone to cut the skin and flesh from their quarry. But it was not until the Stone Age, and perhaps even the Bronze Age, that the knife became a weapon. Over the centuries the knife has changed, but its use has not. To an outdoorsman a knife at times is an indispensable tool. I would rather go on a wilderness trip without a pair of pants than without a knife.

Essentially, outdoorsmen's knives can be divided into two general types: sheath knives, sometimes called belt knives, and folding knives, also called pocket knives. These terms are easily understood. Sheath knives are carried in a sheath, usually on the belt. The blades of folding knives fold into the handle. Some longer and heavier folding knives are also carried folded in a sheath.

Folding knives are nearly always general-purpose knives. They have no specialized tasks. Sheath knives, on the other hand, come in different styles and are for different purposes. The most common is still a sort of general-purpose knife, but we also have filleting knives with long, thin, flexible blades; skinning knives with broad curved blades; caping knives with thin, fine blades and blunted points for caping or skinning out the heads of big-game animals. There is a special dressing knife with a short blade and a heavy knob on the point for dressing big-game animals which lessens the risk of puncturing the intestines. You can even buy an Eskimo oo-you, a skinning knife with a semi-circular blade.

Moreover, when one considers styles; shapes of blades; styles, shapes, and materials of handles; types of steel; and methods of man-

---

◄*The knife is one of man's earliest tools. To an outdoorsman, a good knife is an indispensable piece of equipment.*

ufacture, the choice is staggering and at times bewildering. Choosing a knife is not difficult once you have established some basic criteria. By far the most important consideration is the knife's purpose. The next may be cost. The third criterion may be personal preference — the style of the blade or design of the handle. To some people, this criterion may be even more important than that of cost.

But the most important factor when choosing a knife is quality. Often the high price of an item is not necessarily indicative of a good product. In the case of knives, however, it generally is. There is a big difference in quality between a fine, custom-crafted knife made by one of two dozen custom knifesmiths and a $4.95 knife that you may find at the sporting goods counter of a discount department store.

Signs of good quality are not always easy to detect in knives. In sheath knives, look at the way the handle is attached to the blade. Bolt rivets running through the handle are an excellent way of keeping the handle firmly attached. A bolt which is part of the knife blade is also excellent. Beware of embellishment on the blade. It is useless and may have been put there to distract the purchaser from flaws and poor quality. There should be no gaps where the guard meets the blade. The finish should shine. The lines should be clean and smooth. The knife should feel and look solid, even if it is a delicately bladed caping knife.

A good hint of a knife's quality lies in its sheath. A manufacturer or maker of a good knife will not supply it with a sheath of poor workmanship and quality. However, not all sheaths of high quality knives are practical for field use, so choose one that can stand wear and tear. When you see what appears to be a good quality knife in a cheap and shoddy sheath, don't gamble. Leave it alone.

A good quality folding knife is easier to recognize than a sheath knife. Look for a smooth spring action when the knife is opened and closed. The blade should click audibly into the open and closed positions. When a folding knife is closed, the point of the blade should be covered by the sides of the handle. When the blade is opened, the blade should not move from side to side. Such a movement indicates a loose pivot rivet. The handle, or rather the covering on the folding knife's body that serves as a handle, should be firmly attached. If it looks rather flimsy, don't risk buying it.

To fully understand the underlying features of knives, one should know a little about how knives are made. Essentially a piece of good steel of about one-percent carbon content is heated until it is a bright, glowing red. It is then quenched in a liquid bath. The fluid in the bath varies from maker to maker. The next step can vary. The blade is either forged or milled, depending on what the maker believes produces a superior blade. Outstanding knife makers such as Randall, Moran, and Ruana insist on forging, while equally outstanding knife makers such as Seguine, Olsen, and Gerber mill away the excess metal. Both techniques make good knives. The important point in producing a knife is the tempering of the blade. All high quality knives are well tempered.

When buying a knife, don't take much stock of promotional propaganda such as "special alloys", "miracle steel", and so on. High-carbon steel is high-carbon steel. High-carbon stainless steel is as good or almost as good as plain high-carbon steel, but it is more difficult to work with. This is one reason why in two knives of the same quality, the knife made of stainless steel will be more expensive. Stay away from inexpensive stainless-steel knives.

The type of steel used by the various makers and manufacturers of knives varies. Randall uses Swedish high carbon. American, German, or British high-carbon steel is just as good, but the Swedes are famous for their steel so it is part of the image. Ruana uses a chrome-vanadium alloy. Buck knives have a fair amount of chromium in them which makes them rust-resistant. Morseth makes his knife blades laminated — a hard edge with softer steel on the sides of the blade.

One of the best and easiest ways to ensure that the knife you buy is good, is to purchase knives made by well-known knife makers. Essentially there are four classes of knife makers. First there are the custom knifesmiths. The knives that these men make are entirely hand made, sometimes requiring up to twelve hours of highly skilled hand labor for a knife with special features. Needless to say, custom knives are expensive but, in my opinion, they are well worth the investment for an outdoorsman who uses a knife regularly. A good general-use, custom-made outdoor knife by a top knifesmith can be purchased even today for about $50. Top custom knife makers are Randall, Moran, Draper, Boone, Cooper, Hibben, Loveless, Morseth, Seguine, Carey, and others. A comprehensive list of knife makers and their addresses can be obtained from A. G. Russell, P.O. Box 474, Fayetteville, Arkansas 72701.

In many cases you can obtain a general-use outdoor knife from these people on short notice. Most likely they will have what you want in stock. However, if you want a knife of your own design or with some special feature, you will have to wait — up to eighteen months in some cases. Most knife makers are far behind in their orders. Despite the seemingly high prices, custom knife makers don't get rich — the profit margin is too small and the price of skilled labor is high. Many of them have alternate sources of income. Sequine, the Alaskan knife maker, finds that the only time he can make a profit is in winter when he can hire help at a reasonable price; Randall, the Florida knifesmith, owns orange groves and other enterprises; Carey, the custom knife maker in the fishing village of Port Stanley on Ontario's shore of Lake Erie, is a machinist.

The second class of outdoor knives is made by production manufacturing techniques. Their prices, of course, are lower than those of the custom makers, but their knives are also of good quality. Buck, Olsen, Gerber, Browning, Colt, and Puma are well-known makers of such knives. Browning and Colt are distributors, and who actually manufactures their knives, I don't know. Prices start about $15 for the smaller models and run to about $45. What surprises me is that Gerber and Buck can turn out knives of such good quality at such low prices.

The next class of knives are true mass-production knives, but good quality is still maintained. Such knives will cost from about $10 to $15. They are a good buy for a man who feels that this is all he can afford. Respected brand names of such knives are Marble, Case, Western, Schrade-Walden, and Normark.

The quality control of production or mass-production knives is not as high as that of the custom knife makers, who carefully inspect knives during every stage of their manufacture. Thus it is at times possible to buy a mass-produced knife that has slipped through the quality control and is below standard. When this happens, you can pretty well count on the manufacturer to give you a replacement. These manufacturers stand behind their products, but the manufacturers of the really cheap knives never do. If they did, they could not stay in business.

WHICH KNIFE FOR WHAT?

As I said earlier, the ultimate choice of an outdoor knife depends on its purpose. A canoe tripper or a small-game hunter will find a knife with a three-inch blade ample for his needs. Such a knife will be useful for most chores he will have to perform. A three-inch blade is quite long enough for making a fire stick from a dry white pine bow, for dressing out a game bird, or for cleaning a fish — even a fifteen-pound lake trout.

Such a kinfe can be either a sheath or a folding knife, depending on personal preference. There are several fine folding knives on the market with blades of that length. However, one of the problems with folding knives is that they are usually carried in the pocket where they can be lost easily. Also, the sturdier and heavier folding knives are too heavy and bulky for pocket use. For this reason, some folding

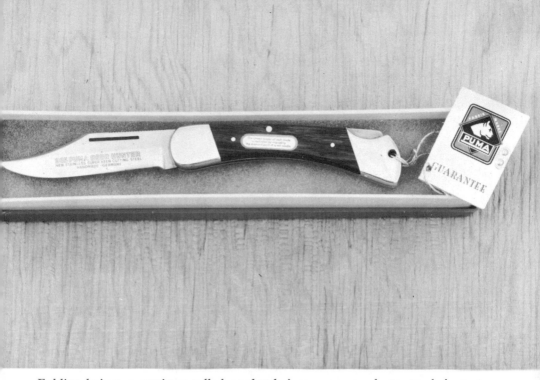

Folding knives, sometimes called pocket knives, are general-purpose knives. A large-bladed folding knife is a good bet for the all-around outdoorsman.

knives do come with a belt case, which is an excellent idea. Another good idea is to attach a leather loop to a snap swivel. A belt is run through the loop and the snap swivel is attached to a ring or keeper on the knife, providing, of course, the knife has one. Should the knife fall out of your pocket, the loop and swivel will prevent its loss.

For wider, but still general outdoor use, a knife with a four-inch or four-and-a-half-inch blade is more versatile. Such a knife will perform almost anything that the smaller bladed knife will and then some. True, you may feel a bit foolish dressing out an eight-inch brook trout with such a big knife, but on the other hand, a four-and-a-half-inch blade is long enough for filleting a twenty-pound northern pike. It also is a bit better for dressing out a moose or an elk; not that a three-inch blade won't do the job in a pinch. I know that it will, because I have done it more than once. But a four-and-a-half-inch blade is a better choice. In fact, for dressing moose and elk, a five-inch blade may be even better. However, in my opinion, a blade longer than five inches is not needed. Any woodsman will tell you that the mark of a greenhorn is a long-bladed knife.

Of course, for special tasks, you should have a special knife. The most common specialty knife for an outdoorsman is a filleting knife. Such a knife should have a long, flexible blade. Although the flesh of a fish is soft and easy to cut, a filleting knife must be able to take a sharp edge. Filleting a fish is actually a fairly precise task. Another specialty knife is a skinning knife. Such a knife generally has a broad, curved blade. Basically it is designed for skinning fur-bearing animals. For skinning deer or other big-game animals, a skinning knife is not really needed. A caping knife, as was explained earlier, is a specialized skinning knife used for caping out the heads of big-game animals. Generally caping knives have broad, thin blades. Although any small-bladed knife can be used for caping, the special knives make the job easier and perhaps present less of a risk of nicking through the headskin. The average outdoorsman does not need a skinning or a caping knife. On the other hand, a big-game hunter who usually hunts without a guide may find a caping knife very handy if he ever bags a head of mounting size.

Every well-designed knife has a certain visual excellence. The design may be fairly conventional, as in the Ruana or Buck knives; it may be subtly classical, like the Morseth deer knife; or very contemporary, like the knives of Gerber. But beyond the looks, there is also a feel. A knife must feel comfortable in your hand. If it feels awkward and clumsy, don't buy it. Look for another design or style.

One thing I would advise is that you avoid too many gadgets on your knife. My remarks here are directed more towards folding knives. Scissors, screwdrivers, and the kitchen sink may be fine for a knife designed for the Swiss Army, but such a knife is not really needed in the outdoors. Usually gadgets on such knives do not perform the tasks they were meant for, or at least they don't perform them well. I prefer a pair of good scissors in my first-aid kit and a set of small and handy screwdrivers with my gun-cleaning equipment. The only gadget I think is useful is a bird-gutting hook, seen on some of the European folding knives.

Aside from knife design, consider the handle. Handles contribute to the feel and the look of a knife, as well as to the overall design. Knife handles are made from exotic woods, staghorn, Micarta, leather, metal, synthetics, and even ivory. I have even seen knife handles made from the feet of the small European roe deer. Such handles give me the willies. They were not meant for outdoor use — for wet or even, at times, blood-covered hands.

Any of the other materials I have mentioned make suitable handles. Those on Buck knives are made of epoxy. Gerber knives have cast-aluminum handles. When I first heard of them I thought they would be slippery when wet or when grasped by a wet or bloody hand, but

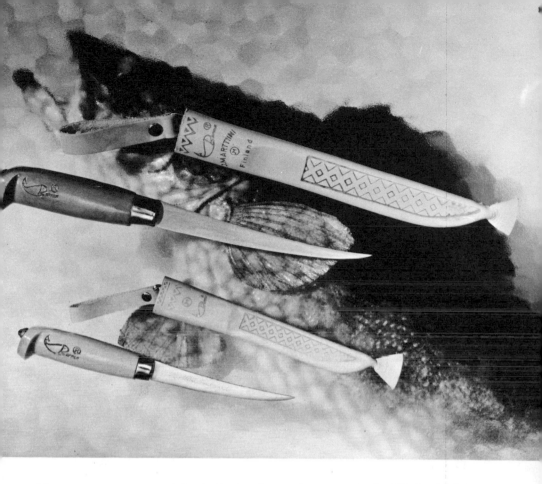

The most common specialty knife for the outdoorsman is the filleting knife. Certainly every angler should have one.

this is not the case. These handles are well designed for a solid grip under all conditions. Randall makes knife handles according to the customer's preference — from ivory to leather. Leather, wood, and staghorn are probably the most common materials for knife handles. They are all good when well made, and they all look good.

HOW MANY KNIVES?

You may need more than one knife — a knife for each major task. This, of course, depends entirely on what you do or want to do in the out-of-doors. A canoe tripper may need only one knife. A folding knife with a three-inch blade or even a sheath knife with a four-inch blade will do. The same applies to campers and hikers. A small-game hunter will never need more than one knife — one with a three-inch blade. A deer hunter would find such a knife adequate as well, unless he wanted to cut through the rib cage and quarter the animal. A larger, heavier knife would be needed for this purpose, but a light ax, hatchet, or meat saw would be even better. A big-game hunter should have a knife with a four-to-five-inch blade and possibly a caping knife. A fisherman should ideally have two knives — one for dressing fish and one for filleting. However, both tasks can be performed with a thin-bladed knife with a four to five-inch blade.

From this we can see that an outdoorsman with many interests may need three or even four different knives. Indeed, when going on a long trip into the wilderness, one should carry a spare knife for general use. More knives are lost than ever wear out or break.

KNIFE CARE

A knife is easy to care for; with proper care any knife of good quality can last a lifetime. It should be stored in a dry place, but never in its sheath, because the leather may have impurities in it which can cause corrosion pits on the blade of the knife. When a knife is being stored for a long period, its blade should be lightly oiled.

Whenever a knife gets wet, it should be dried as soon as possible. This includes stainless steel knives. Water does not do wooden or leather handles any good at all. For this reason, dirty knives should be cleaned with a wet cloth, but not actually immersed in water unless absolutely necessary. Another major sin is the actual misuse of knives. Knives are meant for cutting. They are not meant to be used as hatchets, screwdrivers, or can openers. You cannot expect a knife to keep a proper, let alone a sharp, edge, if you mistreat it.

SHARPENING A KNIFE

A dull knife is a useless knife. A dull knife is also dangerous — more strength has to be exerted to make a dull knife cut, sometimes causing it to slip. A cut with a dull knife is more hazardous than a cut with a sharp knife because a dull knife tends to tear a wound, destroying more cells and making a wider gash that takes longer to heal. The cut of a sharp knife is finer. Less tissue is destroyed. The cut doesn't bleed as much, heals faster, and is less prone to become infected.

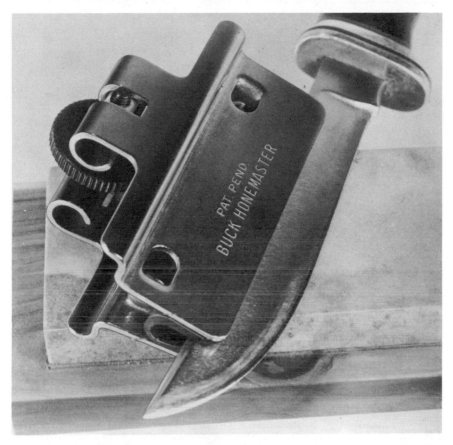

A dull knife is useless and dangerous. Sharpening a knife is not at all difficult. All you need are medium and fine oil stones. A gadget such as this Buck Honemaster makes the task even simpler.

A properly cared-for knife is never allowed to get too dull. A very dull knife is much harder to sharpen, and its edge will become ruined much more quickly. Sharpening a knife is not difficult. A hard-bladed knife may take longer to sharpen, but it stays sharp indefinitely. A knife with a soft blade sharpens quickly and becomes dull just as quickly. A soft blade is a mark of a cheap knife.

When sharpening a knife, there are two considerations to take into account. Are you just touching up the edge or are you putting on a new edge? The latter should be done on a table, bench, or some other firm support, and on a big oil stone. Touching up can be done in the field and usually with a small pocket stone.

To sharpen a knife, lift the back of the blade so that the blade is at a twenty-degree angle. Now stroke the blade across the stone from the back to the point, first on one side and then on the other. Bear down on the knife with some force, but make sure that you maintain the twenty-degree angle. Light strokes will not achieve much. You may think that you are sharpening a knife that way, but you are not. When the edge no longer reflects light and you can shave a hair off your arm, you know that it is sharp. For those who feel that sharpening a knife is a difficult task — despite these instructions — Buck makes a handy gadget which clamps onto the blade to maintain the proper angle. With this gadget the blade is then swept across the stone.

If your knife produces a "wire edge" (you will see it when you hold the knife up), you will need to hone it on a strop or on a piece of heavy cardboard. Just draw the edge backwards across the strop or cardboard on both sides of the blade until the "wire edge" disappears. For touching up an edge, hold the knife and lightly run the stone over the edge at a twenty-degree angle, but don't bear down.

For touching up, any small, pocket carborundum stone is fine. For real sharpening, a big oil stone is needed — at least eight inches in length and preferably twelve inches. The oil stone must be firmly anchored to the bench. The stone should have a medium and a fine side. Be sure to use plenty of light machine or honing oil or some other lubricant to prevent the pores of the stone from sludging up. A. G. Russell's Arkansas oil stones are the best I know. With a little experience you will find that sharpening a knife is not at all difficult.

Outdoorsmen generally think of knives as mere tools, something they work with. And like every craftsman, they take pride in their tools. But is this all there is to knives? I think not. There is something stronger here, invisible and perhaps a bit mystical. It is one of those atavistic feelings that comes from deep in a man's soul. The knife was one of the first implements that separated us — made us different — from the other animals. It contributed to making us what we have been and what we are.

Chapter 9

The Art of Axmanship

I enjoy chopping wood. Why exactly, I don't know. Probably it is a symbolic sort of satisfaction, a spiritual rebellion against our mechanical age. It is unlikely that the kids playing street hockey outside my window as I write this, will ever know how to use an ax. When my father was a boy, one of his daily chores was to bring in a bundle of kindling for the kitchen stove and the stove in the parlor. By the time I was in my teens, when you wanted the house to be a little warmer, you turned up the thermostat. Yet I learned to use an ax despite the handicaps of modern life. I recognized early that axmanship was synonymous with, and a part of, woodsmanship. I believe more strongly than ever that anyone who calls himself an outdoorsman, but doesn't know how to use an ax, is a sham. For those of you who grew up with a thermostat and an oil furnace instead of a wood stove, but want to learn how to use an ax, here is how.

CHOOSING AN AX

The first step in learning to use an ax is to choose a proper one. My recommendation for all-around outdoor use is a single-bitted ax weighing about three pounds, with a thirty-inch handle. Stay away from axes that are much heavier than this because they are meant for heavy-duty wood chopping and little else. Also stay away from two-bitted axes — ones with two blades. They are loggers' axes. The three-pound ax I am recommending can be used not only for chopping wood, but also for driving tent pegs and for dozens of other chores around camp. If weight is a factor, you can go to a lighter ax, two-and-a-quarter or two-and-a-half pounds, with a shorter handle of about twenty-four inches. Such an ax is a better bet than a hatchet. It will do everything that a hatchet will and more, but a person of smaller, lighter build may find a smaller and lighter ax

79

more manageable and more comfortable to use.

When buying an ax, don't skimp on quality just to save a couple of dollars. That is poor economy. When choosing an ax, sight along the blade to make sure that the handle is not warped or that the blade is not set off too much from the center line of the handle. Make sure that the head is attached securely to the handle by being firmly wedged.

Look the handle over carefully. Make sure that the grain runs parallel to the sides. Avoid axes where the grain in the handle twists too much. This could mean serious structural weakness. The best ax handles are made of hickory. Never buy an ax with a completely painted handle. Paint can hide flaws and weaknesses in the wood. Remember, an ax will last a lifetime if you take care of it. Your choice should reflect this.

Every ax should have a leather sheath for the head, not only for safety, but to prevent nicks on the cutting edge. Most axes, when they are bought, have too thick a blade and the cutting edge has too quick a taper to cut well. It should be ground down a little. If you do this on a power grindstone, keep the blade cool by dipping it continuously in a bucket of water. If you let it overheat, you will draw or ruin the temper. An ax can be sharpened quickly on an emery wheel, but eventually this ruins the blade. Coarse sharpening can be done with a fine file. Then switch to a coarse stone and finish sharpening with a medium stone. The best stone for ax-sharpening is a round one. It has no sharp edges to rub through a packsack, so you can carry it with you whenever you take the ax. An ax should never be left lying around. It can cause accidents or accidents can happen to it. Keep it hung in its sheath or sink the blade into the top of a stump.

The handle of the ax is its weak part. At home it is easy to replace — all you have to do is buy a new one, drive the stub out of the ax, insert the new handle, and wedge it firmly onto the ax. But if your ax handle breaks deep in the bush, that is a different matter. Stones and hardwood pegs may be used to drive the broken stub of the old handle out. If this doesn't work, you will have to burn the stub out. Bury the ax head up to the eye in loose earth. Build a fire around it and keep burning until the stub burns off and becomes loose enough to be driven out. To improvise a temporary handle, use any hardwood. To drive the sap out of green wood to toughen it, roast the wood in warm coals. This will season it somewhat.

◀*Every ax should have a leather sheath for the head, as well as a file and coarse stone to keep the edge sharp.*

Every outdoorsman should know how to use an ax. Axmanship is still synonymous with woodsmanship.

CUTTING WITH AN AX

Now, let's fell a tree for firewood. The best wood is a dead, standing tree. It is dry — seasoned — and will burn well. Dead trees and branches lying on the ground are generally damp and make smoky fires. First, walk around the tree to determine which way it leans. That is the direction you want to drop it, because it is easier. If there is a standing tree in that direction that might hang it up, then plan to drop it slightly to one side. Consider also the direction of the wind. It is much easier to drop a tree with the wind than into the wind. Dropping a tree cross wind represents no major problem unless the wind is very strong.

Before starting, make sure that there are no branches, small saplings, or brush within reach of your ax. They could deflect your ax and cause an accident. The secret in cutting with an ax lies in the grip. Grasp the helve — the old term for the handle — with both hands close together near the butt. Touch the blade of the ax to the tree to get the right distance. As you raise the ax over your right shoulder, slide your right hand up (providing you are right-handed) about three-quarters of the way towards the head of the ax. As you bring the ax down, slide your right hand down the handle until it touches your left hand. Strike so that the blade cuts into the tree at about a forty-five degree angle to the grain. Don't attempt to put excessive force into the swing. You cannot get any accuracy this way. The fastest chopping is achieved with many fast and accurate blows, not with brute force.

The first notch is made near the bottom of the tree on the side on which you want the tree to drop. Make the notch about half way through. Tyros generally start by making their notches too narrow. Narrow notches make cutting difficult. A good rule of thumb is to make the notch as wide as the diameter of the tree that you are cutting.

Your next notch should be a few (three or four) inches above the first one and directly opposite it. When the tree begins to fall, step away to one side of the cut, not behind it. Should the top branches of the falling tree catch on another tree, the butt may snap and fly backwards several feet. Many injuries have been caused by backward-flying butts.

The next task is to limb the tree. Stand on the opposite side of the tree from which you want to remove the limbs. In this way, if the ax glances off the tree it will glance away from your legs. Work from the butt to the top, chopping at the bottom side of the branches. Limbing goes fastest this way, and it is easier to make the cuts flush with the trunk. The next step is to cut off the crown. On small trees, this can be done with one notch all the way through. Bigger trees may require two notches, opposite one another, with each going half way.

To cut the trunk into usable lengths, simply chop two notches half way through the trunk on opposite sides of each other as before. This is easier than using one deep notch from the top down. You should always stand on the trunk with your feet spread wide and chop between your feet. To split these pieces, use the butt section as a chopping block. Lean the chunk to be split against your chopping block and strike a good hard blow on the upper end where the piece is resting. If the halves are still too large, split these the same way into quarters. Don't neglect the larger branches for firewood. Cut these into desired lengths by holding them across the chopping block with one hand and striking them at a slight angle with the ax. The chop should be delivered at the center of your chopping block where the branch is firmly supported. To chop up kindling, always lay the piece to be kindled horizontally across the chopping block, grasp it at the lower end, and strike the top. Once the ax is embedded in the piece, you can slam it down vertically to complete the cut. Never hold the piece to be kindled upright with one hand and chop with the other. That is an easy way to cut your hand.

Chapter 10

Chain Saw Tactics

Chain saws, particularly the small six-and-a-half pound outdoors-men's models, have become widely used tools. There are many reasons for this. The biggest one is that the chain saw can perform many tasks quickly and easily, leaving time to enjoy more leisurely outdoor pursuits.

Obviously, chain saws are taken into the outdoors only where their extra weight and the weight of the gasoline needed to operate them present no transportation problems. I use a chain saw on many automobile camping trips, but I would never take one on a backpacking trip or on a canoe trip. Then my ax goes with me. Indeed, I have an ax handy even when felling trees or bucking logs with a chain saw. So do lumberjacks and pulp cutters who use their chain saws to earn a living. Although I consider myself to be fairly handy with a chain saw, I am far from being an expert. To write this chapter, I have sought the advice of experts on the staff of McCulloch, the chain saw manufacturers.

CHOOSING A CHAIN SAW

Choosing the right chain saw out of the many models available is not difficult, once you have decided on the features you are looking for. After that, it is simply a matter of elimination. Most chain saws use an integral two-cycle gasoline engine for power, dependability, and efficiency. Chain saws driven by electric motors are also available, but these are limited in power and mobility.

There are two types of chain drives available in chain saws — direct drive and gear drive. Gear drives are used mostly by professionals who use heavy chains and want maximum lugging power. Direct drive chain saws are lighter, have fewer moving parts, and are easier to use. Little effort is required to use these saws, as the

fast-moving chain pulls the saw through the log. Direct drive saws are the right ones for outdoorsmen. For the outdoorsman or the casual user, the smaller and lighter weight chain saws are probably the best choice. Saws in the six-pound class (weighing about eight-and-a-half pounds complete with bar and chain) are usually rugged, dependable, and easy to use. Other small saws range from ten to fourteen pounds, plus bar and chain.

Engine displacement is the guide to a saw's power. Saws are available with from 1.5 to more than nine cubic inches displacement. A saw in the two to three-cubic-inch range is a good choice for the outdoorsman. Other factors that affect a saw's available power are the type of cutting chain, sprocket, and guide bar used. A good rule of thumb when choosing a chain saw is to pick the one with the shortest guide bar to meet your average cutting needs. For instance, a twelve-inch bar will cut a twenty-four-inch log in half, with two passes. The chain that comes with your saw is matched to the saw's power output. If you need to replace the chain, always replace it with an identical chain.

Aside from the basic features described above, there are many "convenience" features on today's chain saws. Some outdoorsmen consider easy starting to be an important consideration because cutting can require frequent stopping of the chain saw while moving from one spot to another. Today's chain saws are available with push-button electric starters or a compression-release for easy manual starting.

As the chain moves around the guide bar in its special groove, friction develops, building up heat. A lubricating oil must be pumped into the groove during heating to combat this friction. Automatic oiling during cutting is considered by some to be an important feature, as it requires less conscious effort than saws with manual oiler buttons.

One important aspect of any chain saw should be "feel" or operator comfort. Newer chain saws tend to have all the controls (on-off switch, throttle, oiler, choke buttons, and so on) conveniently located near the handle, and handle vibration has been almost completely eliminated. Operator comfort also includes noise reduction. Most of today's chain saws have mufflers that reduce noise impulses up to seventy-five percent.

Modern chain saws have many other extra features. Whether or

◄*Small, light chain saws are now widely used tools by many outdoorsmen. They may be noisy, but they perform necessary tasks quickly and easily, leaving more time for outdoor leisure.*

not your chain saw is equipped with these, will depend on personal preference and budgetary considerations. Remember, though, that as in the case of knives and axes, quality pays in the long run.

CUTTING TECHNIQUES

Any exposed portion of the chain around the guide bar of a chain saw can be used for cutting. Most cutting is done with the bottom edge of the guide bar, allowing the fast moving chain to "eat" its way through the wood. Cuts made with the top edge of the bar require putting the saw through the wood.

To fell a tree, make your first cut (1) to about one-quarter to one-third of the tree's diameter. Then make the diagonal cut (2) to meet the first cut. Begin your backcut (3) on the opposite side, about two inches higher than the level cut.

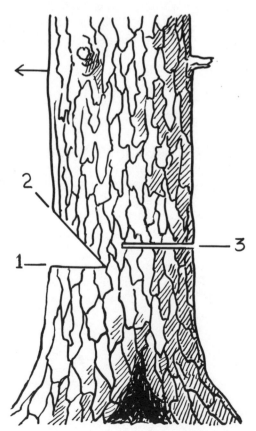

Here is a brief rundown of chain saw cutting methods.

Felling   The method of felling a tree is influenced by physical factors such as the size of the tree, the slope of the ground, adjacent trees, and so on. Experience in felling can be gained by observing professionals and by practising on smaller "safe" trees. Large trees, or those where the direction of fall is critical, should be left to experienced fellers.

When felling a tree, and indeed in any chain saw operation, one should always bear in mind the safety aspect and take no risks; know beforehand your path of retreat as the tree begins to fall; check for dead branches or loose sheets of bark that might fall from the tree; and clear any obstacles from the ground under the falling tree.

Undercutting   Make the first cut horizontally on the side of the tree in the direction of the fall. Consider how much stump you want to leave. Cut through a quarter to a third of the tree's diameter, perpendicular to the line of fall. Then make a diagonal cut downward to meet the first cut. Remove the chunk of wood from the notch.

Backcutting   Start the backcut on the opposite side of the tree, two inches higher than the level of the horizontal undercut. Do not cut through into the notch. Leave a small uncut section between the undercut and the backcut to act as a hinge. The tree should fall at ninety degrees to the face of the hinge. Leaving the hinge thicker at one end can usually make the tree fall toward the thickest side of the hinge. Always remove the saw from the cut before the tree falls, or the saw may get damaged.

Wedging   Wedges are used to control the direction of the fall of a tree and to prevent saw binding in both felling and bucking. Wedges are made of plastic, aluminum, magnesium, hardwood, and steel. Never use a steel wedge in the same cut with a chain saw. The chain can get damaged if it accidentally cuts into the wedge.

If a tree is large or has no apparent lean, wedges are employed to induce a lean. After the undercut notch has been made and the backcut is about one-quarter finished, stop the saw, leaving the saw in the cut. Then drive the wedge into the cut behind the bar. (Two wedges may be needed on large trees.) The wedge must be driven in squarely, in line with the direction of the fall, and not at an angle. Restart the saw and continue cutting. This procedure should establish a lean in the tree. If it has not, stop the saw again and drive the wedge in farther. Be alert! As soon as the tree starts to tip, turn the saw off, pull it out of the cut, and quickly move away from the tree on your preplanned path of retreat.

Limbing   After a tree has been felled, its limbs and branches must be cut off. Start at the butt end and work towards the top of the tree. Branches on the down side of the tree must be cut carefully, as most are under pressure from the weight of the tree. When cut, they can release like a spring and snap in any direction.

When a branch is supported at both ends (by the tree at one end and the ground at the other), topcut the branch first to prevent binding. Then finish with an undercut. When a branch is supported at one end only, undercut first and then topcut. These procedures prevent peeling of the bark by the branch as it falls away. Be sure that the log itself cannot roll or shift as supporting branches are cut.

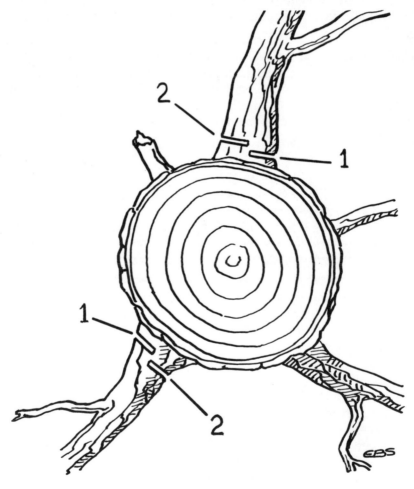

In limbing a tree, if the branch is supported on the ground, make a topcut (1) first and then undercut (2) from below. On branches that are free, make the undercut (1) followed by the topcut.

Bucking The word "bucking" means to cut logs or large branches into convenient lengths. Care should be taken not to cut into the ground on the "blind" side of the log. For logs supported at only one end, undercut one-third of the diameter and then finish from the top. For logs supported on both ends, first cut from the top to about one-third of the diameter and then undercut to finish. Be careful when doing this, as the two halves can drop very suddenly. When bucking on a hill, stand on the uphill side.

With a little practice, you should be able to handle a chain saw with no problem whatsoever. One very important thing to remember, though, when using a chain saw is that there is *no* way to stop a falling tree. Don't start a job you are not certain you can handle.

CHAIN SAW SAFETY

Accidents with chain saws can happen in the same way as accidents with other power tools in your home. They are generally the result of horseplay or other foolish behavior. And they can be prevented simply by treating the chain saw with respect, by wearing proper clothing, and by developing sensible operating habits.

When you are using your chain saw, think safe; plan ahead; keep children away; dress properly (watch any scarves or loose, hanging garments); handle fuel safely; keep your chain sharp; practise preventive maintenance; and stop the saw when you are not cutting. If you observe these basic safety rules, chances of having an accident are minimal.

Chapter 11

Campfire Mystique

Cooking on a campfire is a vanishing art. Indeed, building a truly fine campfire is a skill rarely possessed by outdoor recreationists who probably consider themselves "outdoorsmen". The reasons for this are understandable and lamentable. Undoubtedly a gasoline or propane stove is at times more convenient. Even the young Cree-Indian fishing guides in northern Canada more often than not cook for their clients a shore lunch of fish fillets on a gasoline stove. The old-timers sneer at this, preferring instead the traditional campfire.

Were it not for gasoline and propane stoves, camping would have to be seriously curtailed in many areas of this continent because there are just not enough dead or living trees to go around. To compound this problem, in some areas campfires are not allowed. A campfire has a mystical aura that no propane stove or tent heater will ever match. It symbolizes the very heart of the out-of-doors. Surprisingly, there is a revival of interest in campfires. Perhaps the increasing number of canoe trippers, wilderness backpackers, hunters, and anglers who want to get away deep into the bush may account for this surge of interest. A few years ago many of the camping articles in our outdoor magazines dealt with how to buy camp stoves. Today, they describe campfire woods and how to build campfires. There has always been a hard core of hunters and fishermen to whom a campfire has never lost its charisma, but by and large the rise of interest in campfires and fireplaces is a new phenomenon. I hope that it continues. Everyone who considers himself an outdoorsman should know how to make a good campfire.

◄*Campfires have a mystique that no gasoline stove can match. Somehow the campfire is a symbol of the out-of-doors.*

93

CAMPFIRE WOODS

One way to get a proper campfire is to use the right wood. If you want a pot of tea in a hurry, you will have to use a quick-starting wood such as poplar. But to broil a venison steak, you will need hot coals such as those produced by seasoned hickory.

Wood (and trees) can be divided into two groups — hard and soft. In the case of trees, this division is somewhat of a misnomer. Conifers are called softwoods, while deciduous trees are called hardwoods by forest workers from pulp cutters to forestry engineers. Although all evergreen trees have soft wood, so do many species of hardwood or broad-leafed trees such as poplar, alder, and basswood. The hardwoods with truly hard wood are oak, hickory, maple, birch, and sweet gum.

THE HARDWOOD OR DECIDUOUS TREES

Alder   The alder is a fast-growing tree of swamplands and stream bottoms. It is found from Alaska to the Gulf coast, from Newfoundland to the mid-west, and from the Rockies to the Pacific. It burns fast, with a quick flame and strong heat, but it also burns out quickly.

Alder tends to spit and snap, so watch for sparks. It is excellent for quick boiling and cooking and is good for baking. Because it burns fast, have plenty of it cut. It makes excellent kindling when well seasoned.

Ash   There are about fifteen species of ash in eastern North America. Their range extends from central Ontario and British Columbia south to Florida. Ash, particularly the red, white, and black varieties that are most often used as campfire wood, live on moist sites.

All ash are heavy hardwoods. They don't make good kindling because they tend to start burning slowly. White ash can be used for firewood green, while red and black ash should be seasoned first. They all throw good strong heat, and produce coals which are ideal for broiling and frying.

Basswood   The linden, as the basswood is sometimes called, is found from Maine to the Dakotas and from southern Ontario to Kentucky. It is very light and soft. When used for fuel, it should be well seasoned. It burns quickly and turns to ash rapidly. It spits and snaps and throws sparks readily, so be careful and be certain the area around your campfire is cleared of humus and dead leaves. Basswood, like all soft woods, is good for boiling and quick cooking.

Birch   The birches — black, yellow, and white — make good firewood. Black and yellow birch are superior to white. However, trappers in northern Canada depend on the hardy white birch to heat their cabins through the long winter. Birches are hard and heavy. Yellow birch is found from New England to Minnesota and from Central Ontario south to Pennsylvania. Black birch ranges from southern Maine and southern Ontario to northern Alabama along the Appalachian Mountains. White birch, sometimes called paper or silver birch, is found from Alaska south through Canada and the Great Lakes states to the Atlantic seaboard.

The bark from all these birches is easily stripped off and makes excellent kindling. Birches burn well even when wet. They start readily, and burn slowly and with an intense flame. The coals retain heat for a long time and are good for frying a steak or simmering a stew.

Beech   The beech is a very hard wood. Its range extends from central Ontario to the Gulf of Mexico and from Maine to Kansas. It will burn when green and give off plenty of heat. Many outdoorsmen rate beech as highly as oak. The coals retain heat for a long time, making them a good bet for frying and broiling.

Hickory   All the hickories are excellent campfire woods, with the shagbark being the best. There is no doubt that hickory is the finest of all campfire woods. The hickories are found in a variety of forest habitats, and their general range extends from Maine and southern Ontario south to Louisiana and Texas.

Hickory sawdust and chips are the best wood to use when smoking fish, ham, or bacon. A hickory-smoked ham is far superior to the synthetic chemical-smoking process used on supermarket hams. Similarly, a good steak — beef or venison — broiled on a thick bed of hickory coals is much tastier than charcoal-broiled steak. It burns with a steady and hot flame, and its coals remain hot for a long time.

Hornbeam   There are two species of hornbeams — the American and the hop — and both are very hard and heavy woods. Indeed, the hop hornbeam is sometimes called ironwood. The range of hornbeams extends from southern Ontario through the eastern half of the United States to northern Florida. They do not burn too well when green, but after being well seasoned, they burn with a steady heat and produce hot coals.

Maple   There are over twenty maple species in North America, but only the hard or sugar maple makes first-rate firewood. It is hard and burns evenly, even when green. It leaves very hot and long-lasting coals for long cooking or broiling.

The soft maples, such as the red maple, burn much like poplar — quickly and easily. They are a better bet for quick cooking, but they should not be used unseasoned because they don't burn well when green.

How does one tell the soft maple from the hard maple? It is easy — by the leaf margins. The lobes on a soft maple's leaf have serrated or saw-like margins, and the underside of the leaf is silvery green. The margins of the leaf lobes of a hard maple are smooth, and the underside of the leaf is dull green.

Oak   There are about sixty species of oaks in North America. Most of them make good firewood, but some have to be seasoned first. Probably the best is white oak, which will start well and burn when green.

The red and water oak should be seasoned first. The oaks are all hard and dense woods that burn slowly and produce hot coals. The only exceptions to this are the willow oak and the scarlet oak, both of which burn fast. They can be used for quick boiling, while the other oaks are a good bet for long cooking and broiling.

Poplar   The poplar family contains the aspens and the cotton-woods. They are rapid growing trees. Some of the species are the first trees to recolonize old burns. Some species grow on high, dry, and sandy soils. Poplars range from Newfoundland to Alaska through the Rocky Mountain states, the Great Lakes, into New England, and south to Kentucky.

Poplar wood is light and soft. It burns quickly when dry. It is also a good wood for fast boiling and cooking, and it is ideal for getting a brown sheen on biscuits in a reflector oven. When dry, it makes good kindling.

Sweet Gum   This bottom land tree is a beautiful sight in the autumn. It is found from Connecticut to Florida and west to Texas. It has a fairly soft wood and burns quickly, thus it is best used for quick cooking.

THE SOFTWOODS OR CONIFERS

Balsam Fir   The balsam fir lives on moist bottom lands. Its range extends from Newfoundland to northern Alberta and south through the northern Great Lakes states to the Atlantic seaboard. It is very soft and resinous, with a high moisture content when green. It is difficult to start a flame when green, hence it should be used only when seasoned. It burns quickly when dry and throws a fast heat. It spits and snaps while burning, so be careful. The balsam fir is basically a quick-cooking wood. Small, dry, pencil-thick branches make good kindling, even when broken from a live tree.

Cedar   The outdoorsman should concern himself with only red, white, and western red cedar for campfires. However, cedars are only third-rate as campfire woods. White cedar and western red cedar live on moist sites, while red cedar prefers open areas. Cedars, as a group, are widely distributed over North America. All cedars are light and soft woods that do not burn well when green. When seasoned, they ignite and burn quickly, but still give off a lot of smoke.

When cedar burns, sparks pop and fly, so the campfire must be in an area well cleared of debris and humus. Cedar bark, when dried and shredded, makes tremendous tinder for starting fires.

Douglas Fir　This large western evergreen is not really a fir, but is related to the spruces. It ranges from southern British Columbia to central California and as far east as Montana. It is a soft and light wood that burns quickly. It tends to be smoky. It is suitable only for quick boiling.

Pine　The pines are widely distributed on the sandy soils of this continent. They are light and soft woods. White, red, jack, and lodgepole pines burn well even when green. Pitchpine has to be seasoned to burn well. Pines all throw a surprising amount of light and are generally easy to ignite.

The pines are for quick cooking. They tend to pop and throw sparks, so be careful. They also blacken cooking pots. If you are using pine as a campfire wood, coat the outside of your pots with soap for an easy cleanup before putting them on the fire.

Spruce　The spruces are widely distributed evergreen trees. White and black spruces range from coast to coast and from Alaska to the Great Lakes. Western white, Douglas, Englemann, and Sitka spruces are western species, while red spruce is found from Nova Scotia through New England to central Ontario. The spruces are light and soft. To be good campfire fuels, they should be seasoned. They start easily when dry and make excellent kindling, but they never burn as fast as some of the other softwoods, hence they are a good bet for all-around campfire cooking, as long as hot, long-lasting coals are not needed. Small dead branches of standing spruce trees make good fire starters, even in wet weather, but they do throw sparks.

Tamarack　The larch, as the tamarack is sometimes called, is the only conifer that sheds its needles every fall. There are several species of larch. The larch belongs to the pine family, but is a much better firewood than the pines. Tamaracks range from Newfoundland north to the Yukon and south into the Rocky Mountain states, the Great Lakes states, and into New England. It lives on moist, boggy soils. Its wood is the densest and heaviest of all the conifers, and is best when seasoned. Many northwoods outdoorsmen prefer the tamarack for firewood over all the other species except perhaps white birch. The larch burns with a strong and even heat, and is fairly long lasting, but it doesn't leave as good coals as the birch. When burned green, it spits and sputters.

FIREPLACES

The second secret to a good campfire, particularly a good cooking fire, lies in the fireplace. The type of fireplace you should build depends on the terrain, weather, prevailing winds, and, of course, the length of time you will be using the campsite. The best fireplace is one with a high back for draft and wide arms for pots and pans, and a metal grill or grate. Such a fireplace can be constructed only if there are plenty of the right kind of rocks around.

The next best fireplace is the keyhole or flask-shaped ring made of rocks. The fire is maintained in the main portion of the fireplace. Hot coals are raked periodically under the grate into the narrow, lower portion for cooking. Still another fireplace is a double row of rocks with a foot of space between them for the fire. A grate is placed over these rows to support cooking utensils.

If no stones or rocks are available, a trench fireplace is a good bet. You must dig deep enough to get into mineral soil. The depth also depends on the size of the fire. The trench fireplace should be dug like a narrow, army foxhole. It must be narrow enough for a grate or iron rods, and the open end should be upwind. A more sophisticated version of a trench fireplace has a small hole upwind which is connected with the firepit. As warm air rises from the fire, cooler air comes into the firepit through this hole, assuring better combustion. A fireplace can also be made of two logs — preferably green hardwood. The logs are simply laid parallel to each other about a foot or so apart, or they are laid in the form of a narrow "V". The V-shaped fireplace is better on windy days in open country.

For a quick pot of coffee or tea water, an open fire is generally adequate if there is no wind or if the fire is sheltered from the wind. Three rocks can be used to support the coffee pot. So can three metal tent pegs. The pot can also be suspended over the fire with two sapling forks and a crossbar. Only the tyro will use a perfect fork. The experienced outdoorsman knows that such a fork is hard to drive into the ground. Select a sturdy sapling with a strong offshoot branch. Such a crotch is easier to sink by hammering on the main stem. The forks and crosspiece should always be cut of green wood, if possible.

For cooking over a campfire, you do not need any special cooking utensils. A frying pan is a must, as are a couple of pots. You may wish to add a coffee pot as well. If weight is no problem, a cast-iron skillet is good to have. It must be well broken in before you actually use it for cooking.

For those who want to specialize in open fire cooking, a Dutch oven is a good investment. This is simply a large metal pot — cast-iron or aluminum — with a close-fitting lid and three short legs. I prefer cast iron, but aluminum is much lighter and does not need to be broken in before it is actually used. A Dutch oven is ideal for cooking stews, beans, pot roasts, or even for baking bread over an open fire. You actually put the oven on the hot coals or even bury it among them. For more heat, hot coals are put over the lid. It is easy to cook a stew in a Dutch oven — just bury the pot in hot coals in the morning and the stew will be cooked and waiting for you when you trudge back into camp in the evening.

A reflector oven is still another cooking utensil you may wish to buy. Basically this is a small aluminum lean-to. It is placed by the fire with the open front facing the fire. It is a good idea to build a reflector wall of logs, rocks, or a sheet of aluminum foil on the oppo-

The secret to cooking with fire lies in the wood and the construction of the fireplace. There has been a revival in cooking over campfires in the recent past.

site side of the fire to capture even more heat. A good cook can bake just about anything from a bluebry pie to biscuits in a reflector oven. Most reflector ovens are made of light sheet-metal and fold bake just about anything from a blueberry pie to biscuits in a reflector oven can be made from aluminum foil stretched over a frame of green sticks. The way to build it is exactly like a canvas or a green-bough lean-to that you would build as an emergency shelter except, of course, that the reflector oven is much smaller.

One thing that frequently perplexes the modern cook accustomed to cooking on a stove where temperatures can be regulated, is how to regulate heat. Basically, cooking over a campfire requires constant vigilance. You must check the food constantly so as not to overcook it or burn it. However there *is* a rough way of determining the temperature of a fire which may be of some help.

Hold your open palm in the same spot where your pot will be and count — count "one and one, one and two, one and three," and so on to achieve one-second intervals. If you can only hold your hand there for "one and one" or not even that, you have a fire of over 500° F. If you can hold your hand for two or three seconds, you have a fire of about 450° F, plus or minus ten percent. If you can hold your hand there for four or five seconds, you have about 375° F plus or minus ten percent; six to eight seconds, 300° F plus or minus ten percent.

Cooking over an open fire is a skill that separates the tyros from the experts. It is something that every outdoorsman should learn. One does not have to be a gourmet cook, simply skillful enough to put together a hot and nourishing meal. But it has never ceased to amaze me what culinary delights some campfire cooks can come up with. The old log-drive cooks were like magicians; they could cook an entire meal in two or three Dutch ovens.

Even people who do most of their outdoor cooking over a propane stove may find a basic knowledge of campfire cooking useful. Propane and gasoline stoves have been known to break down.

Chapter 12

The ABC's of Canoeing

Every summer thousands of people, particularly young people, discover the simple but rewarding joys of the canoe. Canoeing has never been more popular. The rivers of Canada's north, which have not been canoed since the days of the fur-trading brigades a hundred years ago, are today being paddled regularly. The urge to get away from it all, the canoe seen as a romantic symbol of rivers flowing free, of wild and unspoiled places, are reasons for the sport's growing popularity.

The canoe is a highly versatile craft. It can be paddled, poled, and some can even be rowed. It can be sailed or propelled by an outboard motor mounted on a side-bracket or a square-stern. It can be quite a tricky craft requiring an expert hand, or, by clamping on outrigger pontoons, it can be transformed into a boat that is safe enough for young children to handle.

CHOOSING A CANOE

Basically, choosing a canoe boils down to three things: the design of the canoe (this means the type of canoe as well as its various features), the length or size of the canoe, and the material from which the canoe is constructed. The purpose of the canoe largely determines its type and size. On the other hand, the choice of construction material depends largely on the qualities desired and, of course, personal preferences.

The standard canoe of today is a double-ender, with the ends lower and the floor flatter than the canoe of yesteryear. The flatter floor makes it more stable with a good load capacity, yet one that paddles and handles well. The lower ends allow it to catch less wind. Another basic canoe is the square-stern. This type of canoe is preferable to the double-ender if an outboard motor is to be used a great deal. There are two types of square-sterns. In the more common one, the entire stern is vertical or square. The other type, frequently referred to as the Y-stern, flares up to form a vertical stern only above the water line. The paddling qualities of the square-stern are inferior to those of the double-ender, particularly in fast water. But in the case of the Y-stern, the sharpness of the stern is preserved under water, hence it paddles as well as the true double-ender. Its only handicap is that the transom can accommodate only a small motor — a three horse power probably being the safe limit, while the more common type of square-stern can accommodate a much larger motor, even a twenty horse power on a big freighter canoe.

There are two other basic types of canoes. The racing canoe, designed for competitive sport, is a long lean craft. It is available in various lengths, some as long as twenty-four feet with a very narrow beam of twenty-six inches or less. There are also canoes with kayak-like characteristics, again narrow-beamed. These are usually decked, have cockpits, and come in various sizes. Their principal use is in river touring. They have a limited load capacity and hence are not really the best choice for extended camping trips into the wilderness. However, with ultra-light camping gear, they can be used.

There are other specialized canoes such as the wide-beamed Sportspal, which is designed principally with stability in mind. Such a craft is useful for fishermen and hunters who want a light and very stable canoe with a shallow draft. This canoe is a poor choice for fast water because it is difficult to paddle. Its shallow draft also makes it difficult to control in high winds. In spite of its poor paddling quality, the Sportspal can be rowed with great success, and indeed the manufacturer equips it with oar-locks and oars. Another specialized canoe is the ultra-light miniature. At one time these were made entirely of cedar planking by the pioneer canoe enthusiast, Henry Rushton. One of the more famous Rushton canoes was the Nessmuk, a mere ten-footer weighing fifteen pounds, nine-and-a-half ounces, and named after the pioneer canoeist and wilderness writer, George Washington Sears, better known by his pen name Nessmuk.

Today, the Old Town Canoe Company has introduced a fiberglass version of the Nessmuk. This new craft is ten feet long and weighs eighteen-and-a-half pounds. This is a great canoe for a man who wants to follow Nessmuk's bidding and travel alone into the wilderness. The expert canoeist will find the modern Nessmuk a real fun canoe, a pure joy to handle.

Canoeing has never enjoyed greater popularity. Young people in particular ▶
see the canoe as a symbol of outdoor adventures.

Most canoes today have keels. The keel has some important advantages. It tends to stiffen the hull and saves wear on the canoe bottom. For paddling in lakes and slow rivers, the keel helps to keep a straight course. But for river travel where white water is likely to be encountered, a keel is a handicap. A keel-less canoe is much more maneuverable. It responds to paddle strokes much more quickly, making it easier to avoid rocks and other obstructions. Hence the choice of a canoe with or without a keel depends largely on where the craft will be used.

Canoes have been made of various types of materials from Indian birch bark to thin cedar planking, pressed paper, rubber, canvas-covered wood, and, of course, in the last twenty years, of aluminum and fiberglass. Today canoes are made only of canvas-covered wood, aluminum, and fiberglass and even the canvas has been replaced by synthetic fabrics. Indeed, aluminum and fiberglass are probably now more popular than wood and fabric. The main reason for this is that aluminum and fiberglass lend themselves better to assembly-line production than wood and canvas, which makes them cheaper at the retail level.

The best construction material for canoes is a controversial topic among canoe buffs. The reason is that every material has its advantages and disadvantages. Also, every canoe buff has his own prejudices and preferences. Wood and fabric canoes are cooler in summer and warmer in winter than aluminum or even fiberglass. They are much easier to repair than aluminum, or perhaps even fiberglass. This can be a very important consideration on a wilderness canoe trip. Wood is also much quieter than aluminum and a little quieter than fiberglass. Wood and fabric require no built-in flotation chambers to keep the canoe afloat in case it overturns. However, wood is expensive and requires maintenance. A sixteen-foot canoe (wood and fabric) can cost up to a hundred dollars more than a fiberglass or aluminum canoe of the same length. The wood also has to be varnished and, if it is canvas-covered, the canvas must be painted.

Fiberglass is less noisy than aluminum. Also it stays cooler than aluminum in the hot summer sun. Like the wood canoe, fiberglass tends to be more elastic than aluminum and usually will take a harder blow without puncturing. Some canoe buffs claim that fiberglass is smoother — that it slides off underwater rocks more easily than aluminum or fabric. Fiberglass is, of course, largely maintenance free and reasonably easy to patch in the case of punctures. The real disadvantage of fiberglass is that it is fairly heavy, but it is impossible to make a fiberglass canoe that is as light as aluminum and at the same time as sturdy.

Aluminum canoes are also maintenance free, certainly in fresh water. They are fairly rugged, although they may dent. It is perhaps for this reason that many canoe liveries use aluminum canoes. Aluminum canoes can be made fairly light with good carrying capacities, hence many canoe trippers prefer aluminum. But aluminum canoes are generally both noisy and hot.

Next to construction material, canoe size is the most problematical aspect for the novice. For two-man canoe trips of several days to several weeks, nothing under sixteen feet is recommended and a seventeen-footer is even better. Although either size will accommodate two people plus their gear, the shorter canoe may ride too low in the water for easy paddling. If such a canoe is selected carefully, it is still light enough to be portaged by one man and can be car-topped fairly easily.

The small canoes — up to twelve feet — are usually one-man canoes. Because they are easy to car-top, they are popular with fishermen and hunters. Generally speaking, the small canoes are less stable and therefore less safe in the hands of anyone less than an expert. The only exception to this is the wide-beamed Sportspal which, because of its wide beam, will accommodate two men and has great stability.

Canoes of an intermediate length — fourteen or fifteen feet — are usually chosen by the novice who believes that the full-sized canoes are too long for him. However, the intermediate canoes are too long for one man and for a long canoe trip, too short for two men plus all their gear, as the canoe will probably ride too low in the water for easy paddling. A good rule to follow when trying to decide on what length of canoe is: when in doubt, buy the next-longest size.

Canoes much longer than eighteen feet are more difficult to car-top and are harder to portage, particularly where the portages are steep and winding. But of course such canoes have amazing stability, and even when fully loaded, don't draw much water. The giant Rupert House canoes are rarely used for recreation. The only place they are seen regularly is in Canada's far north. These twenty-four-foot square-sterns are still the main means of transportation for the Indians around the Hudson Bay coast.

CHOOSING A PADDLE

Choosing a paddle is not at all difficult. Length is one important consideration. The voyageurs of old recommended that the bowman's paddle should reach from the ground to his chin, while the sternman's should go from the ground to his eyes. The modern canoe tripper is unlikely to choose paddles of different lengths. A compromise length from the ground to the nose is a good bet. The blade should not be wider than four and a half to five inches.

Paddles can be made of several different woods. For rapids and shallow water, hardwoods such as ash, hard maple, and yellow birch are best. These woods can take a fair amount of punishment on rocks, sand, and gravel. Of these, maple is the poorest choice because it has a tendency to warp. Don't leave wet paddles in strong, direct sunlight to dry. This promotes warping and even splitting. For deep, open water, spruce paddles are excellent. They are light and very strong for their weight. Spruce is also the best choice for women or young boys.

LOADING, LAUNCHING, AND LANDING

Loading a canoe is a chore that should be planned a little ahead of time. It is a good idea to carry everything to the water's edge and then systematically load the canoe. If waves are likely to be encountered, the load should be moved a little aft. If the bow is a bit overweight, it will ride up slowly with the waves and a wave may come in and hit it before it goes up.

Aluminum and fiberglass canoes are easier to load because one can load them from a beach by partially dragging them on shore. The main thing is to balance the load by distributing it as evenly as possible. This takes very little ability, only a dash of common sense. A canvas canoe must be loaded while it is entirely afloat, either parallel or at right angles to shore. If there is any chance of encountering rough water, it is a good idea to lash the bundles to the thwarts. Or, a line can be run on the inside of the canoe around each thwart and the gear can be attached to this line with snap swivels. Should the canoe swamp or overturn, valuable gear will not be lost.

Another good idea with rough weather in mind is to put some light poles on the bottom of the canoe and pile the load onto the poles. This will ensure that the gear does not get wet from the bottom due to any water that splashes in. A tarpaulin can be used to cover or wrap the entire load or the important portion of it to keep it dry from the top. When packing, remember that the spare paddle must always be on top and within easy reach, in case it is needed in an emergency. When you see a loaded canoe with the spare paddle buried on the bottom, you know that a couple of greenhorns are off on their first trip. If one of them snaps his paddle on a boulder in white water, he will need that spare paddle fast. But that is one way to learn.

Launching a canoe must be done with specific water conditions in mind. Generally it is best to launch it stern first, but on a stormy lake or in rapids this may be dangerous. Launching a canoe stern first has the advantage of the sternman's being in place to steer the canoe immediately; he often does all the steering. The canoe should be launched approximately at a right angle to shore. The sternman should get in even if the canoe is only half afloat. His weight will bring the bow up. Then he can back the canoe out so that the bow is in water deep enough to float even when the bowman gets in. The bowman now takes hold of the bow, puts one foot into the canoe, and shoves off with the other. With a bit of experience, this maneuver

---

There is no question that the canoe is the quiet and ideal way to see the unused, unspoiled places on this continent.

can be done without getting the feet wet or scraping the canoe. A canvas canoe should never be scraped. Actually, it is unwise to scrape even an aluminum or fiberglass canoe.

One of the key things to remember is to select a good launching spot before you load your canoe. It is very embarrassing to have your bowman leap in, only to have the canoe hang up on a rock because of the weight. When you see canoeists pushing with their paddles to get off, you know that you are looking at tyros.

Landing a canoe is like launching a canoe in reverse. An unfamiliar landing site should always be approached with caution. There are times when a bowman may have to jump out if shallows come up suddenly. It is the bowman's responsibility to watch for boulders and shallows. An aluminum canoe can be run up onto a beach of very fine sand by fast paddling and the sternman bending aft to raise the bow. This will not hurt the canoe, but it should never be attempted with a canvas canoe.

PADDLING A CANOE

There are many strokes that can be used to paddle a canoe. The choice of which stroke to use depends largely on what the canoeist wants to achieve. It also depends on the number of paddlers and their position, but for all practical purposes a canoeist needs to know only about four or five strokes to paddle a canoe satisfactorily.

The bowman always sets the paddling pace, but the sternman has the choice of sides because he has to steer as well as paddle, and it is only natural that he steer on the side which is more comfortable for him. In most cases the sternman should be the more experienced canoeist. In rapids, the bowman must choose where to go because he is in front and in a better position to see.

Normally the sternman and bowman sit, but in white water or rough water they should kneel in order to lower the center of gravity. On launching a canoe or landing, the sternman should also kneel. French Canadian voyageurs and Indians always knelt in their canoes, but their leg muscles were used to this form of exercise. Most of us find kneeling to be an uncomfortable position for long periods. Both the sternman and bowman should have at a moment's notice something soft to kneel on.

It is, of course, the position of the stern seat — set closer to the stern than the bow seat is to the bow — that gives the sternman the steering advantage. The aft position allows the stern paddler to pivot the canoe at its midpoint more easily. To change positions, it is best to land the canoe first. It can be done on water but it takes a little practice. On signal, the sternman kneels and leans forward. The bow-man then backs up, crouching and holding onto the gunnels until he reaches the kneeling sternman. The sternman slides between the legs of the bowman and moves forward. The bowman then takes his new position in the stern and the sternman moves up to the bow. This maneuver is harder to execute with baggage, but it is safer then because a loaded canoe is more stable.

The Bow Stroke   This is the most elementary stroke. It is simple and natural. The trick is not to make it too long. Let us assume that the paddle swings through a hundred-and-eighty-degree arc from the time it is dipped into the water until it is withdrawn. For the first ninety degrees, the paddle is deepest in the water. As it rides up during the other ninety degrees, it lifts water instead of pulling at it. It is no longer contributing much to propelling the canoe forward, but your muscles are working as hard, so take the blade out of the water as it passes your hip. The stroke may not look graceful — it is short and choppy — but it will be much more efficient and less tiring than a longer stroke. It will also allow you to paddle faster. The riverine tribes of Africa use this stroke to great effect in their dugout canoes.

The paddle should act as a lever, with the lower hand being the fulcrum. The trick is to use not only your arms, but to use some of your body weight from the shoulder and arm as well, by leaning in a little. This is done by keeping the upper arm stiff for a fraction of a second as you make the stroke. The bow stroke is used solely to propel the canoe, but it is not used only in the bow position.

The Quarter-Sweep Stroke   This stroke is used by the bowman to help turn the canoe faster than the sternman could turn it alone. Of course, it should be done only at the sternman's request. The bow-man leans forward stretching his arms, and sweeps the paddle in an arc, back until it is at right angles to the craft. The quarter-sweep is much more effective from a kneeling position because the sweep begins further forward. If a really tight turn is needed, the sternman will do a reverse sweep on the opposite side.

Bow Draw   This stroke is used to make the canoe turn or change direction sharply. The paddler simply dips the blade fully in the water and pulls it towards the canoe. This draws the canoe towards the paddle. The paddle is lifted straight up for the next stroke. With this simple stroke, a canoe can be moved sideways very quickly and easily.

Sculling Draw   This stroke is simply a figure eight under water. The lower arm and hand must do most of the pushing and pulling, while the upper hand and arm act as a pivot. This is a very useful stroke in fast water where it is unwise to lift the paddle out of the water.

Rudder Stroke   This stroke is not actually a stroke because the paddle is not used to pull the canoe. It is simply a steering stroke where the blade is rotated from side to side to steer the canoe.

Pitch Stroke   This is one of the most useful strokes for the lone canoeist. The angle of the stroke — its pitch — changes gradually as the stroke is carried out. It is also used by the sternman instead of the bow stroke which would overpower the canoe.

The key element of a pitch stroke is wrist action. The same sweep is used as with the bow stroke, but the wrist is rolled outward. Also, the upper hand is rolled out toward the gunnel. In this way, the canoe will move in a straightforward direction. If the bow tends to wander a little in one direction, the paddler can compensate by pushing out the blade and by moving the upper arm towards himself.

Fishhook Stroke   This stroke is easy to teach, but that is its only virtue. The experienced single paddler soon learns that the pitch stroke is much more efficient in propelling the canoe forward in a straight course.

The fishhook stroke resembles the letter J, and indeed it is at times called the "J" stroke. It is begun like a bow stroke, but this forces the bow of the canoe off the straight course. Thus the paddler compensates by pushing over or doing the draw stroke at the end of the bow stroke to get the canoe on its forward direction again.

The fishhook stroke makes the canoe move in a zig-zag fashion. But since the paddler must in one motion carry out two strokes, he uses up twice as much energy. The pitch stroke accomplishes the same thing but more efficiently. It is, of course, harder to learn.

Indian Stroke   This stroke is sometimes called the hunting stroke because it is meant to be done silently. It is simply a pitch stroke in which the paddle blade is never lifted out of the water, but simply knifed forward on its edge. It is this feature that makes it quiet. There is no splash of blade being lifted out, or inserted into the water and there is no water dripping from the blade.

However, this stroke is quiet only when done slowly. When it, and particularly the forward knifing of the blade, are done quickly, the paddle makes a high-pitched whirring noise that alarms wildlife at surprisingly great distances. Knife the blade through the water slowly and the stroke will be quiet. The Indian stroke is also useful in stormy weather because the paddle can be kept in the water at all times.

The essentials of canoeing consist of loading, launching, unloading, and paddling the canoe. Other skills such as running rapids, coping with wind and waves, lining a canoe down the rapids, or tracking it up rapids are all frosting on the cake. They come with experience. Reading up on the subject may help, but no book can tell a canoeist how to run rapids, because so much depends on a man's reflexes, his ability to make split-second decisions, and even his cool thinking.

There is really only one way to become a good canoeist, and that is to go out and paddle a canoe.

Chapter 13

Archery for the Outdoorsman

Bows are ancient. Archeological evidence indicates that bows were in use fifty thousand years ago and perhaps even earlier. Paintings in Spanish caves dating back twenty thousand years show hunters armed with bows stalking the big game of Europe. When a modern archer draws his bow, he is participating in a sport of ancient lineage. It was only a matter of time until the bow, a weapon of the chase, also became a weapon of war. The English, with their long bows, were great archers. The Japanese, Turks, Scythians, and Genghis Khan's Mongols were all skilled bowmen. North American Indians were good archers as well.

Gunpowder and improvements in firearms brought about a decline in the use of bows and arrows both for hunting and warfare. Firearms became more efficient and easier to use. However, at the turn of this century, archery began to enjoy a revival. By the 1950's archery had become a minor but serious sport. My comments here will be restricted to hunting with a bow; target archery is a competitive sport rather than an outdoor pastime.

There is no doubt that hunting with a bow places limitations on the hunter that do not exist when he is armed with a rifle. But there is an added challenge, an added thrill to using this ancient weapon. For many people bow hunting adds a new dimension and meaning to the hunt.

Today, archers enjoy privileges that gun hunters do not have. They may hunt in areas where the discharge of firearms is illegal and usually they are allowed a much longer hunting season because the bow is regarded as an inefficient way of bagging game. Modern archery is not particularly expensive. A novice will find that $40 worth of equipment is ample for learning the sport. A bow hunter after big game can be well equipped for $150.

The beginning archer will find that drawing, holding, and releasing an arrow demand good physical condition. However, strength alone is not enough without good muscle tone. Almost any exercise that stretches and strengthens the upper body muscles will be beneficial. The advice of Saxton Pope, the father of modern archery, is hard to beat. "Begin with a light bow and work up to the heavier weights as rapidly as possible. Do not shoot too much at first. Muscles will strengthen very rapidly if given a chance, but if they get tender and sore, you will have to quit until they recover."

THE BOW

Wood is the traditional material for bows. However, bone, bamboo, sinew, and leather have all been used, together or separately. Yew, osage, and lemonwood are regarded as the best woods for bows. Today fiberglass has become an important material in bow making. Bows made entirely of fiberglass are virtually indestructible.

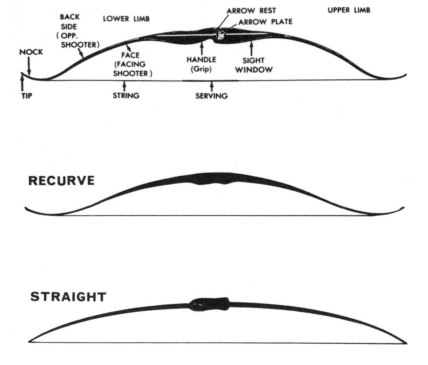

Bows have been made of a variety of materials including bone, bamboo, sinew, leather, wood, and fiberglass. Today, wood-fiberglass laminates are the most popular.

However, bows made of wood-fiberglass laminate are preferred by most archers.

Bows come in three styles — recurved, straight, and semi-recurved. The extra bends on the tip of a recurved bow give it added power and make the bow easier to draw. Recurved bows of wood-fiberglass laminate are the best all-around bet. This type of bow provides the best combination of cast, speed, and stability.

The basic parts of the bow include the upper and lower limbs, the handle section, and the bow string. The handle section has the grip, the sight window, and the arrow rest.

Bow strings are now made of strands of dacron. Each bow string has a "serving" directly across the handle. The serving area has a tightly wound thread around it to protect the bow string from fraying. On the serving is a nocking point, the place where the archer nocks the arrow on the bow string. The nocking point is always located slightly above a perpendicular line from the arrow rest to the bow string.

By far the most important consideration in the beginner's bow is the matter of weight. Bow makers classify their weapons according to the number of pounds of energy required to draw a twenty-eight-inch arrow. The twenty-eight-inch standard is used because the average adult male, properly fitted, uses arrows measuring twenty-eight inches in length. When an archer says his bow weighs thirty-six pounds, he means that it takes that much energy to pull a twenty-eight-inch arrow all the way back. If an archer is an average-sized woman or a small man, the arrows will be shorter, probably twenty-six inches. Here the archer using a thirty-six-pound bow would not really be pulling thirty-six pounds, but his bow is still referred to as a thirty-six-pounder.

The average sized male beginner should start with a bow drawing between thirty and forty pounds, and the closer to thirty pounds the better. For a woman or a boy, fifteen to twenty-five pounds would be a better choice. With such a bow, muscles can be conditioned without strain and the bowman can concentrate on more important matters, besides being able to practise more without tiring. The bow should feel comfortable in the hand, with a full grip. It should be smooth on the draw with a uniform pressure when the string is pulled back and it should be smooth when the arrow is released, without any shocking recoil.

It is important to maintain the proper distance from the bow handle to the serving. This distance is called the fistmele and it is approximately equal to the distance between the bottom of the hand and the outstretched thumb. It can be adjusted by twisting the bow string prior to stringing the bow.

THE ARROW

The arrow is in some ways more important than the bow. It is possible to become a consistent shot with a relatively poor bow if you have good arrows. The reverse is much more difficult. The length and spine are the two major characteristics of an arrow. The length of the arrow is chosen to match the archer. The figure below illustrates how this is done. The arrow length is measured from the base of the pyle, or point, to the bottom of the nock. The length of a broadhead hunting arrow is measured from a point three-quarters of an inch in front of the base of the broadhead to the bottom of the nock. If a choice has to be made between arrows that are a little too short and those that are a little too long, it is wise to take arrows that are a little on the long side.

The spine of an arrow refers to the flexibility of the shaft. The arrow must bend as it passes across the bow. If the arrow has too much spine or not enough, the bow will shoot to the right or the

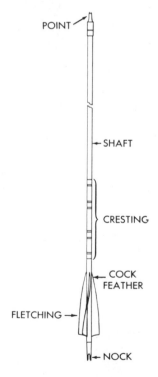

In many ways the arrow is more important than the bow for consistent accuracy.

116

left. Better grades of arrows are matched for weight and spine. They are also matched for the range of bow weights for which they are recommended. Wood, fiberglass, or aluminum are three standard materials from which arrows are made. Wooden shafts are less expensive than fiberglass or aluminum. They are suitable for both hunting and target shooting. They are better for a novice because the tyro archer will damage and lose more arrows than the experienced bowman.

Fiberglass arrows are preferred for hunting because of their ruggedness and durability. Aluminum arrows are preferred for target shooting because they are lighter in weight for a given stiffness in spine. For this reason, they tend to be more precise.

It is advisable for a bow hunter to obtain a matched set of arrow shafts. The target, field, and broadhead (arrowhead) should be matched for weight. In this way the balance and weight of arrows are constant during practice and hunting.

The more common types of points used are illustrated below. The broadheads — hunting points — are about three inches long and one-and-a-quarter inches wide, made of tempered steel. They can have two, three, or four cutting edges which must be honed to razor sharpness to insure proper killing efficiency. There is another type of arrowhead called the blunt. This has a flat face. It is a hunting point for small game who are killed by the shock of the arrow on impact.

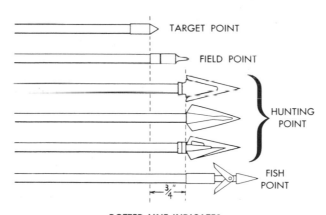

DOTTED LINE INDICATES
ARROW LENGTH MEASURED FROM NOCK

Arrow shafts are made of wood, fiberglass, and aluminum. Arrows come with a variety of points such as the target, field, fish, and several styles of broadheads.

There is also a special arrow called the "flu-flu" designed solely for wing shooting. It is fletched with a fluffy cluster of feathers. This arrow is designed to fly short distances accurately. The head on a flu-flu is designed to transmit shock as well as to cut and penetrate. Shooting game birds on the wing is a sport only for the most skillful of archers.

ACCESSORIES

Bow strings. The best bow strings today are made of dacron-polyester fibers. The novice should buy ready-made strings of suitable length for the length and weight of his bow. Some experienced archers prefer to make their own bow strings. String-making kits can be purchased. Incidentally, the bow is always unstrung when not in use.

Gloves, tips, and finger tabs are three types of protective devices for the fingers of the string hand. Leather finger tips are the most popular, but all three devices are used. They are relatively inexpensive so it is advisable for the beginner to try all three to see which one he prefers and with which he shoots best. The important thing is to make certain that these devices fit well and cause no discomfort.

Arm guards come in two styles. One is a sort of strip guard reinforced with a steel stay and is strapped around the forearm. The other is a leather sleeve which opens under spring tension when it is slipped over the forearm. Both styles are used for hunting and for target shooting. Arm guards are used because a bow string repeatedly slapping the wrist will cause flinching and hence poor release.

Quivers come in several styles — a belt quiver, a plastic bow quiver which attaches to the bow and supposedly has the arrows ready for a quick shot, and a leather-pouch type of quiver which is worn across the back. Again, experience will dictate your preference.

Clothing for archers should be comfortable, soft, and of camouflaged material. The archer needs all the help he can get in stalking within fifty yards or less — dependable shooting range.

Archery requires patience and perseverance, not only when hunting but also to become a reasonably good marksman. Generally bow hunters are above average woodsmen. They have to be, or they will not be successful. I have also noticed that among bow hunters there are few poor sportsmen. The discipline required for archery keeps the less desirable types away from this sport.

Chapter 14

Snowshoes and Snowshoeing

I stopped and looked down over the snow-covered valley. The sun, just rising over the far ridge, hurled its javelins of light onto the snow. It would be a fine day for snowshoeing; a fine day for getting the desk kinks out of my legs. As I tugged at the bindings on my feet to make certain they were secure and had not loosened, I thought of the anthropological heritage of the webbed foot.

In the forested northern regions of the world, the discovery of the snowshoe must rank higher in importance than the discovery of the wheel. The snowshoe made permanent settlement of the northern boreal regions feasible and less precarious. It made it possible for Man to expand and inhabit areas where the snow depth presented an impossible barrier to successful hunting and food gathering.

Snowshoes and skis share ancient common origins. They were first used by the hunting peoples of central Siberia around 4000 B.C. The first instruments were neither snowshoes nor skis as we know them, but rather snowshoe-skis of short, light planks. It is difficult to know when they diverged, forming the webbed foot and the slim ski. But the snowshoe as we know it had its greatest development on this continent, while the ski developed in the Old World.

The ancestors of our present-day Indians brought the snowshoe with them when they crossed from Siberia into Alaska. Without snowshoes, the southward expansion through Alaska would have been difficult. Similarly, without snowshoes, the Athabaskan and Algonquin Indians would not have been able to expand into the northern forested zones of this continent. Before the coming of the horse, the Indian tribes of the northern prairies depended heavily on winter hunts for Buffalo. In deep snow, the bison were very vulnerable to men on snowshoes, who *could* navigate in the deep snow.

The European settlers, notably the French, quickly learned the value and use of snowshoes. The French-Canadian fondness for snowshoes exists to this day. It is doubtful if the northern portions of this

119

continent would have been explored and settled by Europeans as rapidly as they were without the snowshoe. The canoe was the principal mode of travel of the early explorers, but they came for one thing — furs. Without the snowshoe, trapping would have been difficult. Without fur, there would have been no incentive to explore.

Snowshoes are as indispensable to the modern trapper today as they were to the Indian trappers and *coureurs de bois* of old. Every time an outdoorsman dons a pair of snowshoes, he relives this ancient and honorable lineage. His motivation may be different — just a bit of exercise and a lungful of frosty forest air — but an umbilical cord still binds him to the past. The snowshoeing clubs of Quebec still cling to the traditional clothing of the early colonists and *coureurs de bois* on their outings. Traditions die hard.

SELECTING SNOWSHOES

There are essentially five basic styles or shapes of snowshoes. Understandably they have many variations and their names depend on where they are used.

The Algonquin Style This is the most versatile and useful type of snowshoe, and also the most popular. It is sometimes called the Maine or Michigan model. The shape is a classical teardrop with a fairly long tail. The long tail serves to make the snowshoes track in a straight line. It also makes these snowshoes a bit tail-heavy, which helps in keeping the snowshoe's toe up. The Algonquin is the best all-around choice. It is ideal for semi-open forests, but can also be used effectively in heavy bush. It is a good trail snowshoe.

The Pickerel Type This snowshoe is similar to the Algonquin type, except that it is much longer and narrower and has a marked upturned toe. This snowshoe is sometimes called the Alaskan, the Yukon, or the Western model. These snowshoes are fairly big and ponderous, but they are very stable with no tendency to slip sideways. The distinctively upturned toes make it difficult for this snowshoe to catch under a crust or on soft snow. The pickerel is an ideal snowshoe for flat terrain and open woods where no fast turns will be needed. Because of its stability, it is a good snowshoe for a very big and heavy man. It is a very poor snowshoe for thick forest.

◀*When you walk on a pair of snowshoes, you are re-creating an act of ancient heritage. Without webbed feet, the Indians could not have settled the northern forest regions of this continent, nor could the* coureurs de bois, *and later the fur trappers, follow them.*

The Ojibway Type This is a fairly long snowshoe, characterized by a pointed toe or tip, because the frame is made of two pieces of wood joined at the toe and tail. This snowshoe is the easiest to make. The two-piece frame does not require the special steaming to bend the wood that is needed for one-piece snowshoes.

The tip on Ojibway snowshoes is also upturned or flared dramatically. This pointed tip has the advantage of cutting through snow and has no tendency to fill up with snow. It is probable that snowshoes of this style were common among the Indians because of their simpler construction.

The Bear Paw Type This is a "rounded" snowshoe with a broad toe and no tail. The toe is fairly flat. The bear paw is a snowshoe for thick forests, where the snowshoer has to make fast turns around obstacles. Bear paws have a tendency to slip sideways. Because of its wide diameter, it is not particularly good for hilly country.

The Beaver Tail Type This is an oval-shaped snowshoe with no tail, and looks like an elongated bear paw. Its tip is upturned slightly. This snowshoe is frequently called the modified bear paw, the Westover bear paw, or the otter paw. It is a good choice for heavily forested country and, because of its narrower width, it is also a good choice for hilly country. The beavertail is a very versatile snowshoe.

SNOWSHOE CONSTRUCTION

Snowshoes are made of wood with rawhide or synthetic webbing, or of plastic or metal with rawhide or synthetic webbing. All of these materials have their advantages and their weak points. My preference is for the wooden frame. My reasons are probably emotional, at least in part. Wooden frames are traditional. They also require a fair amount of hand labor to make, and in our mechanized age, a man's skill with his hands is something that is rare and should be valued. Wooden snowshoes cannot be mass produced like pieces of plastic.

However, wooden snowshoes require some care. They must be varnished periodically. They should not be exposed to sudden heat, such as the back of the stove, lest they warp. And because hand labor and even wood are costly, wooden snowshoes are more expensive. Good wooden snowshoes cost about $35.

Plastic snowshoes are products of today's technology. Generally

There are five basic styles of snowshoes; their names vary from region to ▶
region.

122

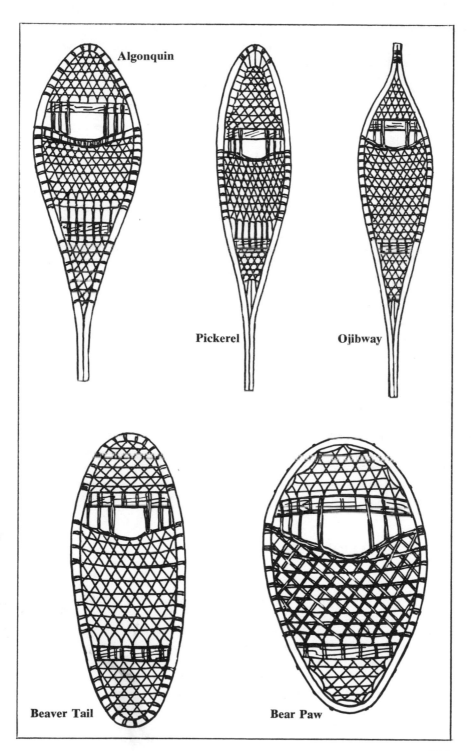

Algonquin

Pickerel

Ojibway

Beaver Tail

Bear Paw

they are made of polypropylene and are cast in one piece. Aesthetically they leave me cold. Some of the earlier models of plastic snowshoes were slippery on crusted ice, but this has been largely corrected. Most of the plastic snowshoes are designed along the bearpaw style, which gives them a tendency to slip sideways. The big advantage of plastic snowshoes is their low price — about $15. They are a good choice for snowmobilers as emergency equipment.

Snowshoes with tubular aluminum frames or even magnesium frames are also available. Aluminum frames have the webbing stamped out of one piece of rawhide, while magnesium frames have webbing of nylon covered cable. Magnesium framed snowshoes are widely used by the military because of their durability. Army people claim that they are virtually indestructible. Aluminum framed snowshoes are extremely light. Many snowshoers like them because of this.

Rawhide, dried untanned hide from which the hair has been scraped, is the traditional *babiche* or webbing for snowshoes. But it is seldom used today. It is harder to obtain and, being a natural product, it is not all that durable. Rawhide rots and deteriorates. Rodents like to chew on it as well. I understand that beaver skins make the best snowshoe rawhide, but moose hides and bear and seal skins are also good. Cowhide, of course, was used most often. The rawhide *babiche* had to be shellacked or varnished regularly to protect it from moisture.

The webbing on modern wooden snowshoes is usually of a synthetic fiber. Nylon fabric with a dense coating of neoprene is generally considered best. The synthetics are superior to rawhide. They are lighter and tougher, they do not rot, and mice do not eat them. Also, once they are stretched tight on a frame, they will not slacken if they get wet. Some of the synthetics look very much like rawhide at first glance.

WHAT TO LOOK FOR

The best wood for snowshoes is white ash. The snowshoe frame should have no knots in it or other defects, and the grain should run straight. The crossbars on the snowshoe should be mortised into the frame tightly and neatly. There should be no sharp edges anywhere that could cut the *babiche* with use and time.

On snowshoes with metal frames, the bends should be smooth and even. If there are welded joints, be sure that they are sound and neat in appearance. This is an indication of conscientious workmanship and tight production standards.

The *babiche*, natural or synthetic, should be tight. The webbing

124

SNOWSHOE SIZE GUIDE

Weight of the Snowshoer in Pounds	Approximate Snowshoe Size in Inches
Bear Paw	
110-130	13x32
130-160	13x34
160-180	14x34
180-200	15x34
200 plus	15x36
Beaver Tail	
110-140	12x30
140-180	12x34
180 plus	12x38
Algonquin	
40-60	9x30
60-90	11x36
90-130	12x42
130-160	12x48
160-190	13x48
190-220	14x48
220 plus	14x52
Pickerel	
110-140	10x48
140-180	10x56
180 plus	12x60

in the middle third of the snowshoe, between the crossbar, should be fairly coarse in diameter. This is where the bulk of your weight will be, so it must be strong. Pay particular attention to the toe guard running just below the toe hole. It takes up much of the shock. The webbing on the toe and heel is generally lighter, made of finer strands.

Many experienced snowshoers have their favorite weave patterns and styles. The coarser weaves are better for dense or crusted snow, while finer mesh is better for loose and soft snow. However, this sort of refinement need not concern you, as most snowshoes today have some sort of "all-purpose" mesh for all kinds of snowshoeing conditions. This is fine for most of us because essentially it is a compromise. But I can see that for snowshoe races one would want the best mesh for the prevailing snow conditions.

The toe hole is an important feature in comfortable snowshoeing. As you snowshoe, the front of your foot should be able to move in and out of the toe hole with each step. Make sure that the hole is wide and long enough for the boots or moccasins you will be using.

The weight of the snowshoes is important. Lighter snowshoes are easier to walk in, more comfortable, and less exhausting, but do not sacrifice lightness for durability. There is a compromise here.

The weight of the snowshoer is also an important consideration in selecting snowshoes. The following table will serve as a guide to matching the weight of the snowshoer to the right size of snowshoes.

HARNESSES

There are several different harnesses available on the market. The problem with harnesses is that a harness of one design is not equally suitable for every type of terrain. I have tried at least five or six different types but I have yet to find one that is good for all snowshoeing conditions.

The most common binding, and the one I frequently use, is a combination of a wide toe strap, a strap around the heel, and a strap over the instep. All of these straps have individual buckles for tightening and adjusting. There are a number of variations of this type of harness. Of the commercially made harnesses, this type is the best.

The old-time trappers and woodsmen used nothing but a length of lampwick which went around the heel and a piece of leather band for the toes. This is surprisingly effective, although you have to get accustomed to it. Of course, today you have to go far into the bush to find coiled lampwick that you can buy by the yard, but nylon webbing works just as well, even if it is not quite as romantic.

One of the most effective snowshoe harnesses is made from the inner tubing of tires. There are two types of these "homemade" harnesses. One simply consists of a wide leather toe strap with a strong rubber band cut circularly from a heavy truck tire tube to serve as the heel strap. To put it on, you simply insert the toe of your boot under the toe strap and stretch the band over your heel and under the toe of your boot, but across the leather toe strap.

The big advantage of this type of harness, aside from its low cost, is that you can slide out of your snowshoes with a twist of your boot. This is a good safety feature when you have to cross ice. Many trappers and woods workers use this type of harness solely because of this. I may, indeed, owe my life to this type of homemade harness.

Some years ago when a Cree Indian trapper, whose trapline I was inspecting, broke his back and suffered severe chest injuries, I took off to get medical help. To make time, I recklessly crossed lakes and swamps that I would most certainly have avoided under normal circumstances. My foolhardiness was exactly that. When crossing a wide beaver pond, I broke through the ice. The fact that I was able to twist my snowshoes off quickly saved my life. After drying myself off by a big fire, I was able to retrieve my snowshoes (which had floated up) with a long pole and so continued my mission of mercy. The trapper, incidentally, survived.

Another type of tube harness and a more sophisticated one is made entirely out of an inner tube, including the toe strap. This is an excellent harness, particularly when made from heavy gauge truck-tire inner tubes. The accompanying diagram shows how this

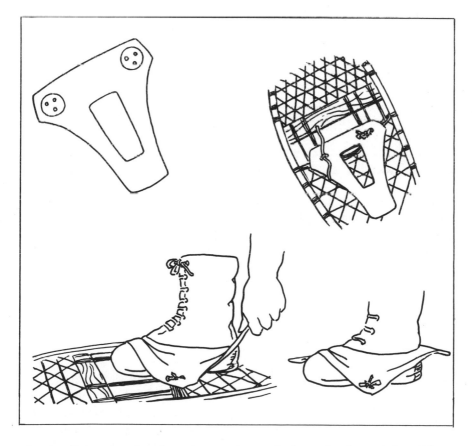

An excellent snowshoe harness can be made from tire inner tubes. Those of heavy-gauge truck tires are best.

harness can be made. A snowshoe with this harness is just as fast to get off your foot as the one I was wearing during my mishap, but this harness is superior, particularly when hills have to be climbed.

FOOTWEAR

Choosing the right kind of footwear for snowshoeing ranks close in importance to selecting the right snowshoe. High Indian moccasins are hard to beat. The main reason for this is that they lack heels and, ideally, footwear for snowshoeing should not have heels.

All kinds of footwear have been tried and used by snowshoers — insulated rubber boots, packs with rubber bottoms and leather uppers, and even rubber overshoes. The best of these contemporary types of footwear are snowmobile boots. Their felt linings are warm and allow for the toe strap to be well tightened without creating any discomfort for the toes. However, their big advantage is the lack of heels on most snowmobile boots, particularly the economy priced boots. No doubt the reason why these boots lack good solid heels is because the designers do not expect the users to do much walking.

OUTER GARMENTS

There is no "best" clothing for snowshoeing. The type of weather expected dictates the type of clothing. I prefer to wear clothes in layers so that I can take off extra clothing, such as shirts or sweaters, and put them on as the temperature dictates. Trousers of tightly woven wool are best. I like parkas or anoracks that are windproof. These can be worn unzipped when the weather turns warm. Two pairs of thin wool socks are better than one pair of thick socks. The traditional headwear has always been a Quebec toque of brightly colored wool. The toque may be a bit warm at times, but its serviceability is unquestionable.

OTHER EQUIPMENT

For traveling on slopes over crusty or packed snow, crampons (spiked, iron plates) are indispensable. They can be taken off and put on like automobile tire chains. Many dedicated snowshoers make their own crampons, and some of the commercially sold snowshoe harnesses have crampons built in. In emergencies, when I had to climb steep hills while running compass lines in timber cruising,

I have even lashed short and sharp twigs to the bottom of my snow-shoes for better traction.

Some snowshoers use staffs while snowshoeing to help them on hills and to give them better balance. Ski poles make excellent snow-shoeing staffs. In hilly country, an ice ax can be very useful, particularly when a longer handle is mounted on it with a ski-pole basket attached at the lower end. This implement can be used as a staff and as an ice ax.

The only other things that snowshoers should carry are: some stout cord, some electrical tape, and a folding knife. Any of these items might be needed to make emergency repairs on snowshoes and harnesses while in the bush.

TIPS ON TRAVEL

Walking on snowshoes is as easy as walking on bare ground. No training period and no practice are needed. This is one advantage that snowshoes have over cross-country skis. The beginner, the first time on snowshoes, will reach surprising proficiency after the first dozen paces. About the only thing a neophyte snowshoer should keep in mind is to remember to pick up his foot and move it over the edge of the stationary snowshoe, and place it down ahead of the other snowshoe. Snowshoeing does not require any sort of cumbersome gait with the feet abnormally far apart.

In breaking trails over new soft snow, the snowshoer should keep the tip of his webs free of snow. The toe should ride high. The way to do this is to take shorter steps. Snowshoes with long tails and up-turned tips have a built-in advantage. Sooner or later every snow-shoer falls. Generally this happens on slopes or when a snowshoe catches on small stubs, fallen saplings, or other debris on the forest floor that lie buried beneath a blanket of snow. A snowshoeing staff or companion is handy at such a time to help you up. But neither is essential. Just make sure your snowshoes are on a horizontal plane and kneel on them to stand up. If you have a staff, you can use it to support yourself. Small trees can sometimes be useful. A companion can give you his hand and pull you up. And in extreme cases, you may have to unbuckle your harnesses and move your snowshoes under you to form a solid platform.

Snowshoeing up or down hill requires a bit more experience. If the slopes are not steep, you can snowshoe up normally. Taking a short run, grasping saplings or brush, or using a staff can all help. Steeper slopes can be traversed by making diagonal tracks across the slope, just as in cross-country ski touring. The length of the zig-zags will depend on the steepness of the slope. Snowshoes should be edged so that they are on a horizontal plane. This is not as easy as with skis because the snowshoes are wider. However, it is not at all difficult. Certainly the narrower models are better for this.

Making turns on snowshoes is much easier than on skis. You simply move one foot in the direction you want to turn and swing the other in front of it. The tips of the snowshoes move the greatest distance, while the tails just pivot. To make a sharp turn, one snowshoe is turned 180 degrees, and when it is solidly on the snow, the other is brought around beside it.

Downhill travel can be done in several ways, depending on the steepness of the slope and the length of the hill. Harnesses have to be tight for downhill travel so that the toe of the boot will not slide under the crosspiece on the snowshoe. If this happens, the snowshoer is likely to fall. If the slope is not too steep, you can walk straight down the hill by keeping your body weight slightly back. The tails of the snowshoes should always be firmly planted first. The steps should be deliberate, almost planned.

A snowshoeing staff is handy when walking downhill. Trees, saplings, and large brush can also be used to help you down and to slow your momentum. On hills with no obstructions, one can slide down by sitting or crouching on the back of the snowshoes. The younger snowshoers can also run down hills, and if the drop-off is a short one and the snow is deep and soft, you can even jump. Jumping on snowshoes is fairly easy and, in my opinion, quite safe.

SNOWSHOEING HAZARDS

Snowshoeing over ice can be hazardous. However, a man on snowshoes can cross ice that would break under the weight of a man walking without snowshoes. After all, the entire working principle of snowshoes is that they distribute weight over a wider area.

No one should snowshoe across ice if it is less than two inches thick. Avoid traveling across inlets where a stream flows into a lake. The ice may be thin here because of the current. Boggy ponds can also be hazardous because the ice may be soft and spongy due to escaping gases. Relatively fast-moving streams are also hazardous because of thin ice.

When snowshoeing across ice-covered lakes and rivers, be sure that the ice ▶ *is at least two inches thick. Avoid areas that have fast-moving currents as well as boggy, gaseous ponds where the ice may be thin.*

130

When crossing a lake or pond, loosen your harnesses and use only the boot toe and toe strap to hold your snowshoe on. This makes walking on snowshoes a little trickier. You have to take shorter steps and not lift your snowshoes quite as high. But if the ice does give way under you, the snowshoes can be kicked off instantly. A lone snowshoer should cut a fairly long, slim sapling and carry it by the middle with him when crossing lakes or streams. Again, if the ice breaks under you, the sapling will hold you up.

A group of snowshoers should always have a line with them, at least thirty feet long. This line can be attached to the lead man who tests the ice and breaks the trail when crossing a lake or river. Any ice that does not crack is very likely to be solid and safe. Walking across frozen lakes and rivers safely requires prudence and caution, and a little common sense. Only when a snowshoer is in a hurry or is careless, do mishaps occur.

A snowshoer and a ski tourer in mountainous country should be careful of avalanches or snowslides. Generally avalanches occur after a heavy snowfall on the hard old snow of steep slopes, or when there is a spring thaw. Overhanging cornices of snow on concave cliffs also start avalanches when they fall. Generally avalanches are triggered by shock waves of sound, by a traveler on skis, snowshoes, or snowmobile, or a sudden change in temperature.

Usually in mountain country there are avalanche warnings in the news media, so if you are planning a snowshoeing trip where avalanches occur, listen to news broadcasts. In skiing country, there is a good network of avalanche warnings. Otherwise use a bit of caution. Snowshoe in areas that are sheltered from snowslides.

Snowshoeing is increasing in popularity. It may not be enjoying quite the same sort of boom as ski touring, but more people are snowshoeing today than since the days of old. Snowshoes have some inherent advantages over cross-country skis. First, they are cheaper. Second, cross-country skis are less suitable for working or doing something other than ski touring because you have to use ski poles. In snowshoeing, your hands are free. A snowshoeing staff is not really needed. I very seldom use one. If I need one to climb a hill, I cut a handy branch or a sapling. (Of course, cutting a staff would not be possible in a heavily used winter recreation area, lest the area become devoid of branches and saplings.)

Snowshoes are superior to cross-country skis when traveling in thick bush such as spruce and cedar swamp. They are also superior when a heavy load has to be carried, as well as for ice fishing or hunting. And, of course, snowshoes are easier to use because there is no learning period.

Chapter 15

The ABC's of Ski Touring

One of the finest ways to get out-of-doors in the winter is on cross-country skis. Cross-country ski touring has brought a new dimension to the out-of-doors. In just a few years, it has mushroomed into one of the more popular winter sports. Anyone who loves the out-of-doors in winter will enjoy ski touring.

Cross-country skis are just as silent as snowshoes, but they allow the traveler to move faster and to cover more ground. They are also less fatiguing because they are lighter, and you do not have to lift your feet to move them forward. You can simply slide the ski. Cross-country skis are more graceful than snowshoes.

Many people who take up ski touring are interested in it as sport in itself, but my interest lies in the fact that it enables me to get out-of-doors more easily and more comfortably than on snowshoes. Photography, wildlife study, and bird watching are all possible on cross-country skis. Winter camping using light backpacking equipment and freeze-dried foods is also possible. As I am writing this chapter, two friends of mine are making preparations to go on a moose hunt in northern Ontario on cross-country skis. Norwegian and Finnish hunters use their cross-country skis in winter hunts for ptarmigan, hares, and even caribou. Finnish trappers patrol their traplines not on snowshoes but on cross-country skis. Cross-country ski touring may be relatively new to this continent but, as a sport, it is at least a century old, with its roots firmly embedded in the thin soil of the Scandinavian hills and forests. It is certainly older than alpine skiing.

Traveling on skis goes back many centuries. Skis were invented by the hunting tribes of Siberia and from there spread westward into what is now Scandinavia. The Swedes learned about skis from the Finns and Lapps during the height of the Norsemen era. Skis were used solely as a method of winter transportation — for hunting and for war.

Military training was the springboard for skis as an object of recreation. By the late eighteenth century, skiing became a sport, but it was not until the middle of the nineteenth century that it became popular. Generally Norway is credited as being the cradle of ski touring, and skiing in general. Cross-country ski touring is a far cry from downhill alpine skiing. The techniques are different. The equipment is different. Even the attitudes of ski tourers and downhill skiers are different.

EQUIPMENT

Skis Cross-country skis are longer and narrower than downhill skis. They range from special mountain tourers, which are three inches wide and weigh six pounds, to narrow racing skis that are a mere two inches wide and weigh three pounds. For general purpose ski touring, a ski of about two-and-a-half inches is the best bet. Length is determined by the ski tourer's height. To get the right length, raise your arm straight up over your head and measure from the middle of your hand to the floor. But if you are heavily boned and weigh above average for your height, choose skis in the next length group.

Cross-country skis are made from laminated woods. The better skis have several dozen laminations to prevent warping. The sole of the ski should be of very hard wood, with hickory being the best. The edges of high-quality skis are reinforced with lingostone. Watch for warpage when buying cross-country skis. Lay the skis on a straight bare floor to make sure that they are not twisted or warped. Cross-country skis for general touring cost from $25 to $50.

Boots There are a number of different cross-country ski boots on the market. The main feature that distinguishes these from alpine ski boots is their flexibility and light weight. Special skis also require special light and low-cut boots resembling a track shoe. For general ski touring, a full boot is the best choice. It is warmer and better at keeping your feet dry. Lightness is an important factor to consider when buying boots. Boots made of composition rubber soles vulcanized to the upper parts are the driest. Good, serviceable boots can be purchased for about $20.

Bindings The boots and bindings should be purchased together to ensure that they are compatible. There are essentially two styles

Cross-country skis offer one of the finest ways to get out-of-doors during▶ the beautiful days of winter. It is no wonder that this fantastic sport has risen so quickly in popularity.

of bindings — the cable-around-the-heel and the pin. The pin binding is generally used for racing and requires a boot in which the soles project forward. The binding is attached through a pair of holes in the sole.

The cable-around-the-heel bindings are used for touring and mountaineering. They require a boot with a groove in the heel. These bindings come in two major styles — the Kandahar and the Tempo. Both have their advantages and disadvantages. Tempo is probably the best choice for ski touring, particularly for the beginner. Good cable-around-the-heel bindings can be purchased for about $12 to $16.

Poles Ski poles are made of cane, fiberglass, and aircraft-alloy tubing. The latter are the lightest and most expensive. They are also the toughest. Cane poles are still a good choice. They are strong and light and are the least expensive. Fiberglass poles are also good and cost somewhere between the cane and metal poles. The basket on cross-country poles should be fairly large, particularly if you intend to travel in forested country where snow might be fluffy and loose. The metal tips on the poles should curve forward and should be very sharp. Poles run from about $8 to $20.

Rucksacks or Knapsacks The cross-country ski tourer will need some sort of lightweight rucksack to carry a wax kit, some lunch, a tea pot, some extra clothing, and possibly a camera and film. If he is going on long tours, replacement tips for the skis will also be needed. Rucksacks can be purchased from $6 to $25 depending on size, quality, and material.

Clothing Ski-touring clothes should be light in weight. If you expect to be moving about constantly, then the clothing need not be heavily insulated. The exercise will keep you warm. The thing to avoid is bulky or loose clothing that may catch on branches and shrubs. You should also avoid clothing that will not breathe properly and trap all of your perspiration on the inside.

Knickers are traditional for cross-country skiing. However, light wool trousers are just as good for general touring, particularly in woods. Such trousers are more versatile, but knickers are good because they allow easy movement. A light wool shirt and a sweater are a good combination when used with a light, windproof nylon shell. The choice of undergarments is wide. Fishnet underwear is excellent. Long underwear will not be needed except in very cold weather.

In cold weather a woollen toque is hard to beat but in mild weather it is probably too warm and will cause your head to sweat. A simple headband is adequate then. A balaclava is needed only for extremely severe cold such as that encountered in high mountains. Light woollen gloves are ideal for milder weather, if gloves are needed. Woollen mittens are warmer in cold weather and are just as efficient as gloves. The ski tourer should always wear two pairs of socks — a long thick pair of woollen socks on top of a soft pair of cotton socks. If you intend to wear knickers, the socks, of course, must come to the knee.

Anklets and Gaiters   Anklets and gaiters are the only specialized clothing needed for ski touring. Anklets are worn at all times except in deep, soft snow, where gaiters are better because they will keep you drier. Gaiters should have zippers in the backs so that they can be put on after the boots. The base of the gaiters should have nylon drawstrings or leather straps so that they can be tied under the instep of the boot. The best gaiters are made of soft canvas. Anklets should fit snugly around the top of the ankle and around the boot. They should have elastic for the instep of the boots.

Presuming that one owns a suitable shirt and sweater, the other pieces of clothing for ski touring will cost between $30 and $40. From these costs we can see that one can become well equipped and clothed for the sport of cross-country skiing for about $100. People on limited budgets could even do it for twenty-five or thirty percent less. I have seen skis, poles, boots, and bindings sold as sets for $55 in some of the larger department stores.

TECHNIQUES

The first step is to get the feel of the skis on your feet. Move around. Flex your feet. Pick up the skis by raising your feet. Kneel down. Then begin practising the simple step-around turns by lifting one ski and moving to one side, and then following with the other ski. Coordinate this movement with movements of your poles. Practise this backwards. These exercises will help you to become fully relaxed on your skis.

The Diagonal Stride   The diagonal stride is the basic maneuver in cross-country ski touring. Begin practising your stride on level ground, preferably on a trail broken by other skiers. Move out as if you were walking, sliding your skis at each step. Keep your body straight and erect, and transfer your weight from one ski to another in a smooth, rhythmic fashion. All this is easy. A couple of hours of practice will give you a fair degree of proficiency.

Now, gradually increase your stride by putting more movement into the sliding ski. The easiest way to achieve this is by forcing the forward leg out each time, so that it forms an acute angle at the knee. At first, your legs will tire rapidly because you are making muscles work that are normally unused.

To a degree, the more you make your sliding-ski slide, the stronger your basic maneuver will be. The key to your efficiency lies in developing good rhythm. Once you have achieved good rhythm on your skis, you can go on to the diagonal stride. Without learning this stride, you are really only running on your skis and no one can endure this for great distances or maintain any speed.

The diagonal stride consists of applying force to the opposite pole in order to maximize the slide of the skis across the snow. By having long glides, you minimize movements and energy outputs, hence you lessen fatigue. The poles do not actually exert a great deal of power, but they act as timing and balancing mechanisms. The basic movements are these:

Thrust one leg forward along with the opposite arm, and plant the pole ahead of the foot and about ten inches to the side. Put all your weight on the forward ski as it slides out. As the forward slide begins to diminish, put pressure on the planted pole and draw the rear ski forward as quickly as possible, bringing the other pole forward to repeat the cycle. The whole idea is to increase the length of the glide by kicking with the rear leg. To achieve this, you must learn to maintain proper balance, leaning slightly forward and with the knees slightly bent.

The Kick Turn The kick turn is the basic maneuver for changing direction. It can be done on level ground or on a slope, if the skier is perpendicular to the fall line. The fall line is the shortest line down the hill. To make a kick turn, bring one ski forward and up so that its tail is embedded in the snow half way between the boot and the tip of the other ski. When the ski is almost vertical, it can be rotated and put down facing in the opposite direction of the second ski. The other ski is then picked up and crossed over the first ski, and placed beside the first ski. You have now made a 180-degree turn in direction. Poles are used in this maneuver to help maintain balance. The kick turn is actually quite easy to perform once you have become accustomed to your skis. With the kick turn, you can traverse almost any slope.

Downhill Techniques Sliding downhill on cross-country skis is not at all difficult, but it does require practise and total familiarity with these light skis. For straight downhill running, the best stability is obtained with a wide stance. Poles can be used to help with balancing. It is also best to run downhill with one ski slightly ahead of the other. The same type of crouch can be used as in alpine skiing.

◄*Cross-country skis are as silent as snowshoes, but they allow the traveler to move faster and cover more ground.*

Straight downhill runs can also be done in the telemark position. In this position, the torso of the skier is almost vertical. The forward ski should form a right angle with the leg and the knee, while the knee of the other leg lies close to the trailing ski so that the shin is almost parallel to it. This position is best in soft, windblown snow, when conditions are unpredictable. It is also good over uneven and bumpy ground.

Downhill turns can be achieved by edging or by a step turn. To make an edge turn, the skier simply rotates his ankles so that the edge of the ski will knife into the snow. This will cause him to move swiftly in that direction. When making an edge turn, the skis should be close together to minimize the chances of falling. The poles again are used to help balance the skier.

Edge turns should be practised on gentle slopes first. They are most useful in deep snow. Once you have mastered them, you will find that they are a good way of turning.

The step turn is the basic turn of cross-country ski touring. To make this turn, the skier crouches with his knees bent and his weight on the heels of his skis. He then, picking up one ski at a time, moves to the right or left with short steps. Since with each step he is actually pushing off with the trailing ski, the skier's speed is increased. This is frequently very disconcerting to the tyro. However, it need not be. It is again a good idea to practise the step turn on gentle slopes before taking on steep ones.

To control speed, cross-country ski tourers can use the step turns or Christianias of the alpine skiers, or the snow plow, in which the skis form a V at the tip. For this, the skier should place his weight well back on his heels and bring his knees forward.

There are other downhill techniques that the cross-country skier can use, such as the pole-jump turn, the telemark turn, the ski glosside using the poles to act as brakes on descending narrow trails, and so on, but they are beyond the scope of this brief introductory chapter.

Uphill Techniques   The cross-country skier soon learns that the shortest route is not always the fastest. It is frequently faster to go around a hill than to climb it. Also it is sometimes faster to select longer but gentler slopes on hills. This is much like deciding between shooting the rapids or portaging. Shooting the rapids may save time, but if you swamp the canoe, you will have to spend half a day trying to salvage and dry your gear.

One way to climb a slope is by traversing it. By edging the skis, the ski tourer makes a level track. Diagonal strides can also be used to go up gentle slopes, but the slides must be kept short. Traversing here will also help. On steep slopes, the side step is the easiest. It is certainly easier than the V-shaped herringbone step. In the side step, the ski tourer simply moves up the hill sideways, keeping the skis across the slope. The poles are used for balance and support.

The only other techniques required of the cross-country ski tourer involve crossing obstacles. In most cases, this is largely a matter of common sense and convenience. When crossing bare roads and highways, skis should be taken off and carried.

Every cross-country skier must expect to take falls. Obviously beginners will fall more frequently. One of the secrets of falling is to learn to relax and not stiffen up. This is why professional wrestlers and stunt men seldom ever get hurt, even when they fall. The second thing is to learn to control the fall. If possible, try to fall on soft snow on the side of the trail rather than on packed snow. Falling flat on your face, surprisingly enough, is frequently the safest. The cross-country bindings offer enough flexibility to allow you to fall to the side. Dropping back on your skis may cause a broken ski, but it may be the safest way to fall on steep, brushy slopes.

WAXING CROSS-COUNTRY SKIS

Correct waxing is one of the secrets of cross-country ski touring. Correctly waxed skis allow the tourer to ski down a slope as well as climb a twenty-degree slope without side stepping.

Different snow conditions require different waxing techniques. This presents immediate problems, because snow conditions can change in the course of a day. It is easier to wax for fresh snow than for old, icy snow or wet snow. There are a number of waxing kits on the market, many of which give instructions and have guides for what waxes to use and how. To become proficient at waxing skis takes a fair amount of ski-touring experience and a bit of experimentation. There is no other way around it.

It is impossible to cover all the techniques and methods of ski touring in one short introductory chapter. Anyone who is interested in the sport should purchase a good book on the subject. There are a number of reasonably priced paperbacks on ski touring on the market. One of the best is Edward Baldwin's *Cross-Country Skiing Handbook*.

Chapter 16

The Basics of Snowmobiling

There is no doubt that the power toboggan has revolutionized winter outdoor recreation throughout the northern portion of this continent. Alas, not all its effects have been beneficial. Snowmobiling has had its growing pains. Harassment of wildlife, destruction of young trees, cutting of wire fences, trespassing on private property, and littering, have caused problems. But in the last few years, there have been many indications that snowmobile enthusiasts are showing signs of maturity. Through public education, the formation of snowmobile clubs, and the establishment of snowmobile trails, snowmobile misuse and the poor outdoor manners of snowmobilers have declined.

Although I am not a big snowmobile booster, I do recognize their value. They have opened up vast stretches of the northern woods that no one ever traveled during the winter months. I admit to a preference for snowshoes and cross-country skis, but I use a snowmobile as well. A snowmobile enables me to fish remote lakes. I have also used a snowmobile to carry me quickly into the backwoods, and then snowshoed to points of interest.

The snowmobile has made the work of many woods workers much easier. I know of northern Canadian trappers who can, with a snowmobile, live at home with their families and cover their traplines with ease. It enables them to travel greater distances, spreading out the harvest of raw furs over a wider area. It has even helped to establish humane trapping methods. How? A trapper now can easily carry the big and bulky Conibear traps that kill instantly. This was difficult to do when a man had to walk everywhere on snowshoes.

◄*In its early years, snowmobiling experienced growing pains — trespassing, harassing wildlife, and destruction of young trees; but through education and snowmobile clubs, the sport is slowly maturing.*

Although I know how to operate a snowmobile efficiently and safely, I do not consider myself an expert in the field. To write this chapter, I sought the advice of the snowmobiling experts of the Outboard Marine Corporation, manufacturers of several brands of snowmobiles.

DRIVING A SNOWMOBILE

It takes only a few minutes to master the basic controls of a snowmobile. As all models differ slightly from one another, study the owner's manual for your specific machine before trying the machine out. For a beginner, the best place to practise is in the wide open spaces. Fields, snow-covered frozen lakes, or any other large space you can find that is free of trees and other obstructions is a good place to practise. And as with any form of sport, practice makes perfect. Snowmobiles are in their element *off* the road. Snowmobiling is the most fun after a medium snowfall (six to twelve inches). Extremely hard packed snow or glaring ice make for tricky handling.

Balance and track contact are the two basic things to watch when handling a snowmobile. Once you have these mastered, you can tackle steep grades, traverse hillsides, and twist through wooded areas with your vehicle under total control. During your learning hours, play it safe. The principle of balance is quite simple. On rolling terrain or on the side of a hill, the snowmobile has a tendency to tip. You must be ready to shift your weight to counteract this tendency. For example, if you are climbing a steep slope, you will probably have to lean "into the hill" to maintain balance.

Track contact is the second important consideration. The turning action of the track provides the forward movement of the machine. If the snowmobile banks too far to the left or right, it will lose partial or total contact with the snow surface, and the results will be the same as jacking up the rear wheels of a car. You can apply all the gas you want, but you will not be going very far. You are just spinning the track and not obtaining maximum power.

Snowmobilers have developed three driver positions to attain best balance and track contact. The sitting position is the most common, followed by kneeling and standing. In the kneeling position, the driver places his right knee on the seat and his left foot on the running board. In the standing position, he straddles the seat, placing both feet on the running boards. You should try all three positions and choose the one that gives you maximum control and permits quick shifting of weight.

Turning The most important maneuver in snowmobiling is turning. Turning a snowmobile is a lot like turning a bike or motorcycle. The more you lean into a turn with your body, the sharper will be the turn. One thing to remember when turning is that you have got to have enough power to keep moving. Too little throttle and you will stall your turn. Try a few figure 8's with at least a forty-foot diameter in each loop. Go slowly at first, gradually building up speed on repeated runs until you feel the machine start to "slip" sideways. This can be controlled by either easing off or increasing the throttle opening. A little experimentation will tell you how much power you will need for different snow conditions.

Now try a series of left and right turns along a straight course, like a slalom skier. Just as you found when you first started to drive a car, turning in one direction will be easier. When you find your weak side, practise turning on it a little more than on the other side.

General Riding Tips Most snowmobiles were made to carry two people — the driver and one passenger. The heavier the load on a snowmobile, the less performance you will get from it. When you are cruising in the woods, watch out for tree branches, snow-covered logs or hidden snow-filled depressions, and other hazards that could upset your machine. Dips or holes have a way of becoming nearly invisible during the late afternoon when the light becomes poor. Be careful driving at this time. Use goggles with amber lenses for flat light conditions and smoke-colored lenses for glare light conditions.

Plan ahead. When you drive up a hill, remember that you have to come down that hill too. If the hill is very steep, you should have a good plan as to how to get down. On very steep hills it is a good idea to "traverse" the hill on the way down by making shallow sweeps across the face of the slope, progressing thirty feet vertically with each sweep.

Test the snow conditions before setting off on any trip. What was true of yesterday's snow is not always true of today's. An overnight freeze or snowfall can bring surprises. Before taking off, try a few turns and stops. You will get a better feeling of the trail and you will have more fun.

Lower your speed in unfamiliar territory, keeping an eye peeled for obstacles. If you are riding double, both people must be on the alert to maintain good balance. The person riding behind the driver should be prepared to shift his weight at any time to counteract a lean when crossing rolling terrain.

Traveling on ice and on hard-packed surfaces can be tricky. If the surface is too slick, the track may have difficulty making good solid contact. You can prevent this by starting out slowly and building up speed gradually. If the track starts to slip, retard the throttle slightly and try again. Practise with shifting body weight and the proper use of the throttle and brakes and soon you will have mastered most snow conditions.

BE WELL EQUIPPED

For minor emergencies that may arise, you should be well equipped on any snowmobile outing. You should always carry a tool kit including a spare drive belt, spark plugs, a plug wrench, an adjustable wrench, pliers, a screwdriver, electrician's tape, your owner's manual, and a tow rope.

As on any outing in the out-of-doors, it is a good idea to carry a map of the area where you are snowmobiling, as well as a compass (it is easy to become disoriented on a snowy day), a first-aid kit, an

Snowmobiling has revolutionized winter recreation throughout the northern regions of this continent.

ax, a good-quality knife, and a container of windproof and water-proof matches.

If you plan a long trip strap a pair of snowshoes onto the snowmobile for each passenger. Carry an emergency fuel supply!

A lightweight block and tackle with up to fifty feet of rope may mean the difference between getting your snowmobile going again if badly mired, or abandoning it.

BE PROPERLY DRESSED

Snowmobiling will not be much fun if you are not properly dressed. In fact, improper dress can be a hazard in this sport. Of course your

---

The snowmobiler should be well dressed in a windproof suit, warm boots, gloves, and, ideally, a helmet. Shatterproof snow goggles are also a good, safe way to protect your eyes from sun glare and flying ice.

WIND-CHILL CHART

ESTIMATED WIND SPEED IN MPH	ACTUAL THERMOMETER READING (°F.)											
	50	40	30	20	10	0	−10	−20	−30	−40	−50	−60
	EQUIVALENT TEMPERATURE (°F.)											
calm	50	40	30	20	10	0	−10	−20	−30	−40	−50	−60
5	48	37	27	16	6	−5	−15	−26	−36	−47	−57	−68
10	40	28	16	4	−9	−21	−33	−46	−58	−70	−83	−95
15	36	22	9	−5	−18	−36	−45	−58	−72	−85	−99	−112
20	32	18	4	−10	−25	−39	−53	−67	−82	−96	−110	−124
25	30	16	0	−15	−29	−44	−59	−74	−88	−104	−118	−133
30	28	13	−2	−18	−33	−48	−63	−79	−94	−109	−125	−140
35	27	11	−4	−20	−35	−49	−67	−82	−98	−113	−129	−145
40	26	10	−6	−21	−37	−53	−69	−85	−100	−116	−132	−148

(wind speeds greater than 40 mph have little additional effect.)	LITTLE DANGER (for properly clothed person)	INCREASING DANGER	GREAT DANGER
			Danger from freezing of exposed flesh

Trenchfoot and immersion may occur at any point on this chart.

---

snowmobile clothing must be warm and windproof, and it should be as waterproof as possible. It should also be light and flexible and not too tight. You must have freedom of movement in order to handle your machine properly.

Many people prefer the insulated one-piece suits, snug at the ankles, wrists, and neck. Others find the two-piece suits (coat and pants) more convenient. Insulated boots should be worn, and these boots should be as waterproof as possible. The boots should also have non-skid soles and a drawstring top in order to keep out snow.

A face mask of some sort is essential for sub-zero weather. Face masks come in many varieties and some look pretty weird, but when snowmobiling, comfort comes first. Thermal underwear and socks, and heavy mitts with wool liners will protect you in severe cold. Heavy gloves or mitts are also useful for pushing away branches when driving through the woods.

When operating a snowmobile in especially rugged areas or woods it is a good idea to wear a helmet over a woollen liner to protect your head from injury. The glare of the sun off the snow often dictates the use of tinted, shatterproof goggles. Goggles also protect the eyes against wind and against branches and twigs when driving through wooded areas.

Always try to keep clothing and footwear dry. When you get off your machine to exercise, take care not to get overheated. If you perspire, you will be colder later on. If it becomes necessary, loosen your clothing to allow warm air to escape.

It is extremely important that you do not wear long scarves or mufflers that may leave loose ends flying in the breeze. There is always a chance that these loose ends may get caught in the drive train or the track, with disastrous results.

Watch for frostbite when out in temperatures of zero or below, or even above zero if the wind is strong. Use the buddy system to spot the telltale white spots on the exposed flesh of ears, cheeks, or noses of your companions. Minor frostbites will respond quickly to the thawing effect of a warm hand or other heat. Refrain from rubbing a frostbitten spot, as this may damage frozen skin tissue but will certainly cause severe chapping.

The wind-chill chart on the opposite page will give you an idea of what can happen to exposed flesh under calm wind conditions compared to temperatures with different wind velocities.

SNOWMOBILE SAFETY

Some preliminary precautions to take when using a snowmobile are: stay physically fit; know your equipment; plan your activities in advance; wear proper clothing; check the weather forecast before venturing any distance; and remember that alcohol and snowmobiles don't mix. Staying physically fit is of primary importance because below-zero weather lowers human efficiency and you must always bear in mind that if you break down you may have to walk.

Check the throttle and brake controls on your machine before starting out. Be sure both move freely without sticking. A frozen throttle could send your snowmobile out of the starting gate like a cannon, and it could injure you and others. Check your headlights and tail lights if traveling at night. Carry a flashlight as a backup device.

Be sure you have plenty of fuel. Carry an emergency fuel supply. Travel with other people. Particularly in unfamiliar territory it is good to have at least one other machine with you. In fact, one of the best ideas is to join a local snowmobile club. You will have lots of fun and you can learn from other snowmobilers. If you are pulling a sled or toboggan, use a rigid tow-bar to prevent rear-end collisions on sudden stops.

Do not willfully jump your vehicle. Even the experts have difficulty in controlling machines whose skis and track are air-borne.

When you are a newcomer, whether to the area or to the sport, stick to established trails. Marked trails have been provided in many parks, national forests, and conservation areas for your convenience. By following them, you reduce the possibilities of having an accident or trespassing on private property.

If you get off trails, travel with caution in unknown areas. Snow camouflages many unexpected changes in terrain. Match your speed to the terrain. Traveling too fast over rough snow surfaces increases the chance of unpleasant spills. Tipping over into soft snow may be part of the fun, but a spill at high speed can be dangerous.

Never cross rivers or unknown lakes at night. At all times, use extreme caution when traveling on ice. Currents and weather conditions can make ice unsafe. Breaking through thin ice is a major cause of serious snowmobile accidents. Unexpected skids on ice are also dangerous.

If you stay on marked trails, you will not travel on roadways or railroad right-of-ways. These were not created for snowmobiles and should not be used by them. If it is necessary to cross a roadway or a railway track, stop your snowmobile and make a thorough check for any traffic. Then cross at right angles as quickly as possible. Avoid collisions with other snowmobiles by throttling down at trail intersections and when other snowmobiles are approaching from an angle.

Keep a sensible distance behind other snowmobiles when traveling in a group. Tailgating causes bent skis, broken tail lights, and even personal injuries.

If you become mired in deep snow, be patient. Never take a chance of slipping under the track when pushing the machine with the track running. If others are helping you, do not let them tug on the skis while you run the vehicle. It could come out of the snow suddenly and injure them. If your track needs clearing, do not let anyone lift the tail while standing behind it, while you are running the track at high speed. Projectiles hurling off a spinning track can be extremely dangerous.

Know wind-chill hazards and avoid frostbite. Wear a protective face mask if it is very cold. Numbness is generally the first sign of frostbite. If you feel this condition, stop and warm yourself before the frostbite becomes serious.

Even if you consider yourself an expert at driving your snowmobile onto its trailer, a winch is a much better idea. Many injuries and damaged automobile trunks have resulted from "experts" driving onto their trailers. Once your snowmobile is on the trailer, make sure it is tied down securely.

150

Chapter 17

Give the Cook a Chance

One of the bonuses of such outdoor pastimes as fishing and hunting is fish and game for the dinner table. No store purchase can duplicate the delicacy of a shore lunch of freshly caught walleye or brook trout. No supermarket chicken can compare to pheasant or ruffed grouse. And steaks of moose or caribou broiled over hardwood coals or charcoal on the patio barbecue can be much more flavorful than beef produced in modern feedlots and pumped full of antibiotics and specially designed feed to accelerate their growth.

TAKING CARE OF YOUR CATCH

I learned when very young that the faster a fish is put into the frying pan and onto the fire after it is caught, the better it tastes. Fish, unlike game, does not improve with aging. Of course it is not always feasible or possible to cook fish right after they have been caught, but a shore meal of fresh fish is a delightful part of fishing and the outdoors. Fish deteriorate and lose their fine flavor very quickly after being caught if they are not properly handled. To let any fish deteriorate to the point where it is a poor meal is a shame. It would have been better to let the fish go to reproduce and to fight another day. To let a fine game fish spoil so that it is unfit for human consumption is literally a crime. If you let this happen you are a disgrace to the fraternity of fishermen. Letting fish spoil is against the law almost across the entirety of the United States and Canada.

But it is not surprising that so many fishermen do not like to eat fish. If I treated fish the way they do, I would not like it either. Yet it is almost as easy to take care of fish properly as it is improperly.

One of the worst culprits is the fish stringer. Often by the time the fish are taken off to be cleaned, they have already deteriorated in quality. The warm surface temperature of the water in the summer

FILLETING A FISH IS EASY

1. Make first cut just behind the gills. Slice down to the bone, then, without removing blade, turn it and slice straight along backbone . . .

2. . . . to the tail. Note that the fillet has been cut away from the rest of the fish. After slicing fillet off at tail, turn fish over and repeat procedure on the other side.

3. With both sides removed, you have cut away both fillets without disturbing fish's entrails. This is the neatest and fastest way to prepare fish. Now to finish the fillets . . .

4. Next step is to remove the rib section. Again, a sharp, flexible knife is important to avoid wasting meat. Insert blade close to rib bones and slice entire section away. This should be done before skin is removed to keep waste to a minimum.

5. Removing the skin from each fillet is simply a matter of inserting knife at tail and "cutting" meat from the skin. With the proper knife, like the "Fish 'N Fillet," it's easily done.

6. Here is each fillet, ready for the pan, or freezer. Note there is no waste. Remember not to overwash fillets. This will preserve tasty juices and keep meat in its firm natural state.

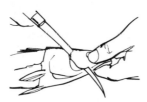

7. Cutting out the "cheeks" is the next important step. Few fishermen know that cheeks are the filet mignon of the fish. Though small, they're tasty and well worth saving.

8. Slice into cheek where indicated then "scoop out" meat with blade, peeling away skin. Repeat on the other side. Many fishermen save cheeks until they have accumulated enough for a real gourmet's delight.

9. Here are all parts of the fish after you've finished. Note fish head, entrails, spine, tail and fins stay intact. This is the neatest way to prepare most game fish and, once you've mastered these few steps, the easiest.

---

months kills and spoils fish quickly. Any fish that struggles for a long time before dying or being killed will not be in as good a condition as one that is killed immediately. A far better gadget than a stringer for keeping fish alive is a collapsible fish keeper made of plastic hoops and nylon netting. In such a sack, fish will live for hours or even days.

If a fish stringer is all you have, do not string the fish through the gill slit. You will injure the gills and the fish will die much faster. String the fish through the lower jaw by puncturing a hole. Do not drag your fish behind your boat at fast speeds, while moving from one spot to another. When you do this to a fish, its gills cannot function. It cannot breathe and so it suffocates.

The best way to keep fish is on ice. That is how commercial fishermen do it, and they manage to keep their fish fresh and firm. In summer, every fisherman should have an ice chest with him, filled with chipped ice. When a fish is caught, it should be killed immediately by rapping it sharply on the head with a stick and then buried in the ice. Ideally the fish should be dressed — gutted and gills removed. Certainly big fish should always be gutted.

Do not let the fish in your ice chest slip down into the melted water. Keep the spigot on the chest open. A wooden rack made of dowelling for the bottom of the ice chest is a good way to keep fish out of any water that may not have drained from the chest.

During the cool spring months, fish can be kept for several hours in the open air. The old-fashioned wicker creel is good for this. It allows air to circulate, but does not expose the fish to the sun. One thing I feel very strongly about is that any fish which is to be kept in a boat or on shore should be killed immediately. It is degrading to the angler, to the sport, and certainly to a fine game fish, to see it flop about and die slowly. Every creature deserves a dignified death.

Cleaning fish is one chore that no one really likes. I do not either. But there is a right and a wrong way to do it, and the right way is generally the fastest. How a fish should be cleaned is determined partially by how you want to cook it. Will the fish be fried, broiled, or baked? The size of the fish also plays a role. For example, the fish may be too small to fillet.

To clean small trout — skillet-sized trout — all you need to do is to gut them, cut the gills out, wash and dry them, and they are ready to cook.

Any fish that you intend to bake or broil whole can be cleaned with a minimum of equipment — a big board, a sharp knife, and a scaling tool. Light cotton gloves are also handy. Fish are easier to grasp with a gloved hand, and the gloves prevent scratches from spiny dorsal fins.

To clean a fish that is to be cooked whole, first scale the fish briskly with a scaling tool. Do this under running water to keep the scales from flying all over your basement floor. But be sure to put a screen in the sink drain-hole to avoid plugging up the drain with fish scales. With most fish, scaling from the tail to the head goes fastest.

Cut out the vent or anus with a "V" cut. Then hold the fish belly down on the board and cut through the spine just behind the head. Don't cut through the entrails of the fish. After severing the spine, push and twist on the head with one hand and pull on the body. The head will come loose with all of the entrails attached. Cut off the fins and wash out the dressed fish. Now it is ready for the pan.

Filleting a fish is also easy. For this you make your first cut behind the gills. Slice down to the bone and, without removing the blade, turn it and begin slicing straight along the backbone towards the tail. Keep cutting all the way to the tail. You will notice that the fillet in the diagram has been cut away from the rest of the fish. After slicing the fillet off at the tail, turn the fish over and do the same thing on the other side. When you have done this, you have cut away both fillets without disturbing the fish's entrails. This is the neatest and fastest way to prepare your fish.

To finish your fillets, you must remove the rib section. Again, you will need a sharp and flexible knife to avoid wasting meat. Insert the blade close to the rib bones and slice the entire section away. This should be done before the skin is removed to keep waste to a minimum. The skin can be removed from each fillet by simply inserting the knife at the tail and cutting the meat from the skin. Start cutting a half inch from the tail end of the skin, allowing a wedge for the best grip. With a proper filleting knife, it is very easy.

You now have each fillet ready for the pan or the freezer. There is no waste. Remember not to overwash the fillets. You do not want to wash away the tasty juices or take away from the fish's natural firm state.

Cutting out the cheeks is the next step. Few fishermen know that the cheeks are the filet mignon of the fish. Although small, they are tasty and well worth saving. Slice into the cheek where indicated, then scoop out the meat with the blade, peeling away the skin. Repeat the same procedure on the other side. Many fishermen save these cheeks until they have enough for a real gourmet's delight. After filleting you should wind up with the fish head, entrails, spine, fins, and tail all intact. This is the neatest way to prepare most fish, and once you have mastered it, it is the easiest.

Catfish have to be skinned. With big catfish, start by making a circular cut not much more than skin deep completely around the fish, just behind the gills. Then make two more skin-deep cuts, one along the back to the tail and the other down the belly to the tail. Take a corner of the skin on the back of the fish with a pair of pliers and pull the skin tailwards with one smooth motion. Now repeat this on the other side. With a bit of practice, it goes very quickly. With real whoppers you may have to use both hands on each side with a pair of pliers in each hand, and you may find the skinning task easier if the catfish is hung by its head.

Skinning and dressing small pan-sized catfish is easy. You should start by placing your knife behind the adipose fin (the small, fleshy fin on the back of the back) and cutting the skin until your knife reaches the dorsal fin. Watch out for the backbone. Continue to cut downwards behind the head, through the fish and right down to the spine, but not through it. Lay the knife down and grasp the head in your right hand (if you are right-handed) and the body of the catfish in your left hand. Bend the head down and break the backbone.

Then insert a finger of your left hand over the end of the spine and into the rib cage and pull firmly. With your right hand, slowly pull the head toward the tail. Do this smoothly and steadily. Do not jerk! The skin will peel smoothly, taking the guts, still attached to the head, with it. Your catfish is now ready for washing and the pan. This technique takes a bit of practice, but it is the easiest way to clean catfish that I know of.

There is no doubt that fresh fish are superior to frozen fish. There is also no doubt that if care has been taken to freeze the fish properly, frozen fish can be exceptionally good. A fish that has been killed and cleaned immediately after being caught, has been kept on ice, and has been frozen the same day, cannot be distinguished by the average person from a fresh fish, as long as the fish has not been kept in the freezer for too long.

Fish, like all meat and vegetable products, should be frozen as soon after harvesting as possible. It should also be frozen as quickly as possible. This is best accomplished by placing fish, once they have been packaged, around the outside of the freezer near the freezer coils and by not overloading the freezer with too much food to be frozen at one time. Most freezers today are quite efficient, and can freeze solidly and very quickly one-and-a half to two pounds of product per cubic foot of freezer space.

Frozen fish should be stored between zero and twenty degrees Fahrenheit to keep enzyme activity to a minimum. Of course fish must be adequately wrapped for freezing to guard against moisture loss and discoloration commonly called "freezer burn". Pack your fish in heavy plastic freezer bags or freezer wrap, carefully eliminating all air from the bag before closing and tying it. Label your packages as to what species of fish they contain, whether they are whole fish or fillets, and the date they were frozen.

Fish can also be frozen in containers made of plastic or glass. This is very handy for small fish or fish chunks. To freeze fish in containers, pack the containers carefully to within one or one-and-a-half inches of the top. It is important to leave an airspace at the top for expansion once the liquid in the container has frozen. Fill the space around and between the fish with a chilled two-and-a-half percent brine solution. The fish must be covered with this solution. Make sure there are no air bubbles in the solution. Now secure the top of the container, making an airtight seal. When the container is placed in the freezer, the ice formed around the fish will keep the flesh away from air and will prevent any loss of moisture. The only disadvantage of this method of storing fish is that the containers take up a large amount of freezer space.

For maximum flavor, frozen fish in plastic bags or freezer wrap should be used within two to three months. Fish frozen in containers filled with brine can be kept a little longer, up to six or nine months. The best way to defrost fish is slowly in your refrigerator. Most fish take about twenty-four hours to thaw. Thawing at room temperature is not a good idea. If you need your fish in a hurry, defrost them by immersing them in cold water. Never refreeze fish.

TAKING CARE OF WILD MEAT

Every outdoorsman should know the basic procedures for dressing and skinning game. It is one of the musts of wilderness survival. A number of factors affect the taste and flavor of wild meat. For example, some game species are tastier than others. Also, the taste of meat frequently depends on the physical condition of the animal, on what it has been feeding, and even on its age. For instance, a bull moose shot during or shortly after the rut is generally in poor condition. The fat that the bull put on during the summer is gone — burned up in chasing cows and fighting other bulls. During the rut, mating, not feeding, gets preference in a bull's daily life. The animal is thin and sinewy, consequently the meat will not be at its best.

But basically the quality of wild meat depends on how the animal was killed and how it was treated immediately after being shot. An animal that has been wounded and then tracked and chased all over the backwoods has its system full of adrenalin and will not be as good as the one that was killed when it was completely relaxed. Also, the faster the game cools off after being shot, the better it will taste. This is true from mallards to moose.

DRESSING BIG GAME

Big game animals should be dressed immediately after shooting. This means opening and emptying the body cavity, thus allowing the animal to cool quickly. This is most easily accomplished by laying the animal on its back with its head uphill if possible. The animal may have to be anchored with rocks placed by its side or with its legs spread apart and tied to trees. Be sure not to touch the musk glands just below the hocks. They are marked by tufts of dark hair. The glands give off an oil with an odor that can taint your hands.

First, the anus and rectum are loosened by cutting in the rump around them and they are firmly tied. A cut is then made in the skin and the abdominal wall from the pelvic bone right up to the rib cage. Cut slowly, with the edge of the knife pointing upwards, working the blade between two fingers which lift the skin and the abdominal wall away from the internal organs as you cut. Make sure that you do not puncture the intestines. Cut around the penis and loosen it at this time.

Loosen the diaphragm, the wall of tissue separating the stomach and intestines from the lungs and heart. This is done by cutting around the diaphragm close to the ribs. In deer-sized animals, you can now reach up and grasp the windpipe and gullet. Cut these off as high as possible with your other hand. In elk and moose-sized animals, you have to split the ribs with an ax or a hatchet to be able to reach the windpipe and gullet. When the windpipe and gullet are cut free, you can strip all the viscera and organs with a strong backward pull on the gullet and windpipe. An occasional cut with a knife will help to free the internal organs from the mesentery tissues as you pull. When you come to the pelvis, finish loosening the rectum by cutting from the inside of the carcass and pulling the anus through. Then drag the offal away from the carcass, keeping the heart and the liver. This basic dressing technique works on all big game animals.

The next step is to wipe up any spilled matter from the intestines and blood from the inside of the carcass. A dry rag is best, but moss or leaves can be used. If you have to wash something off with water, dry the cavity thoroughly afterwards. Meat that is left wet for any length of time can spoil.

You must cut away the musk glands on the hind legs. With a finger and a thumb, pinch and pull up the glands while sliding a sharp knife under them and cutting right along the base. Throw the removed glands away and wash or wipe your hands and the knife before touching any meat. Some hunters prefer to deal with the glands first, before even dressing the animal. This is fine if you are near water and can wash afterwards but, if you are not, it is better not to take a chance on tainting your hands and the knife.

In the very mild weather of early fall, it is frequently necessary to quarter a moose or elk carcass in order to get it to cool quickly. A field-dressed moose or elk (one with its internal organs removed)

is a massive animal. The meat on the animal's back is insulated by the ground and can sour quickly. The best way to prevent this is to quarter the animal and hang it. This is not always necessary in cold weather; however, for the best possible meat it is a good idea to skin and quarter every big game animal while it is still warm. Then place the meat in loose cheesecloth and let it cool. Trim away the badly shot meat or it will cause spoilage.

Of course it is not always possible to skin out big game after every hunt. However, all big game should be kept off the ground after field-dressing so that it can cool quickly. With elk or moose, you have to prop the carcass up with logs and poles, or quarter and hang it. Deer-sized animals are normally hung whole. The carcass should be left hanging for a period of a few days up to as much as fourteen days in a cool, breezy spot. Keep it away from the sun. The length of the hanging period depends upon the temperature. If the temperature is above fifty degrees, four or five days is fine. If the temperature fluctuates between twenty and forty, two weeks is excellent. Beef is best kept in a cold locker at thirty-five degrees for two weeks and ageing wild meat properly is even more important than ageing beef for tenderness. Your meat is then ready for cutting and wrapping for the freezer. You can let your local butcher do this. Deer, moose, and elk can be cut up just like a steer. Trim away as much fat as possible because it is the fat that contains much of the gamy flavor that many people find objectionable.

SKINNING BIG GAME

Skinning big game is not difficult. Generally the legs are cut off below the knee and hock joints. The skin is then girdled and peeled away. The body is skinned out very quickly. In the case of bears, the cuts are made on the inside of the legs and the feet are skinned out, keeping the claws on the foot if a rug is to be made from the skin. This is also done in the case of mountain goats where the hoofs are left attached to the skin. All skinning is much easier when the carcass is still warm. Try to keep the hair away from the meat. The hair of the pronghorn can taint the meat a little.

The trickiest part of skinning big game is around the ·head. This has to be done if the head is to be mounted. If you can have the

---

◄*Big game animals should be dressed as soon as possible after shooting. The faster an animal is dressed and the carcass cooled, the better the wild meat will taste.*

head frozen or can get the head to a taxidermist within a few days, leave it for him to skin out. There is less chance of a mistake or a wrong cut, but if you are going to be in the bush for a couple of weeks, you must skin out the head, particularly on bears, or the hair will start to slip. Skin slowly and carefully, particularly around the eyes and lips. Cut the ears off flush with the skull. Cut the entire snout off where the septum between the nostrils meets the skull. Scrape all the flesh away from the hide and salt the hide well, rubbing the salt in.

EQUIPMENT

Besides a good knife and a honing stone, the big game hunter may also need a hatchet or a light ax, a meat saw, cheesecloth meat bags, and ropes and pulleys to dress his animals and take care of the meat. A light ax is needed for splitting the pelvis of a moose or elk. A meat saw is best for getting through bones and for quartering big game, but the task can also be done with a light ax. Meat bags are needed in warm weather to protect the meat from flies. Ropes and pulleys are needed to get a moose or elk off the ground and out of the woods. The type of game you hunt dictates what type of equipment you need.

DRESSING SMALL GAME

Rabbits and squirrels are very easy to skin while they are still warm. Squirrels, once they are cold, are much harder. The easiest way is to behead the animal and cut off its feet and tail. Then pinch the skin on the back and cut through it, making the cut from the root of the tail to the neck. Stick the fingers of one hand around the carcass, inside the skin, and pull the skin away with the other hand. It is as easy as pulling a glove off a hand. Small game can be field-dressed immediately after shootiing with a technique similar to that for deer or you can wait until the animal is skinned out to dress it.

GAME BIRDS

The diet of game birds influences their taste and flavor. There is a big difference between a mallard and a merganser, and between a mallard feeding on wheat in a stubble field and a mallard in a marsh. But just like big game, the flavor of fowl depends upon how the birds were treated after shooting. The worst thing for game birds is to put

160

them into an air-tight, rubberized game pocket in the back of a hunting jacket, particularly on a warm day. The best place to carry birds is in a game carrier on a belt or over the shoulder, letting air circulate around them as much as possible.

DRESSING GAME BIRDS

There is no doubt that field-dressing birds immediately after they are retrieved is a good idea. It hastens cooling and helps to keep fluids from the punctured viscera out of the body cavity. Such game birds as sage grouse and spruce grouse should be dressed immediately and their crops removed, for the best flavour. It is also a good idea to do this for the species of ducks that eat a great deal of animal matter. With other game birds, it is not as important, unless they have been badly shot. However, it is still preferable to do it right away.

Field-dressing a game bird is easy. First, cut yourself from a branch a bird-gutting hook about the length and thickness of a pencil. The hook portion is made from an off-running branch. Then cut a small slit by the vent and insert the hook into the bird's body cavity. Twist it around three or four times and pull out the entrails. Some European folding hunting knives have a bird-gutting hook on them — a wonderful idea. The detailed cleaning is done later.

The field-dressing can be done more easily with your hands. If you are near water, that is fine. It takes only a moment to wash your hands and continue the hunt. Field-dressed birds can be left hanging in a cool, breezy place for several days without deteriorating in flavor. Refrigeration is needed only if the birds are to be kept a week or more in mild weather before being eaten or frozen.

SKINNING GAME BIRDS

Some hunters prefer to skin their birds, mainly because it is easier. However, to us purists, skinning game birds such as quail, ruffed grouse, pheasants, mallards, and canvasbacks is a bit of blasphemy. Skinning removes much of the fine flavor, particularly if the birds are to be roasted. The birds also dry out more when cooked. However, if the birds will be cooked in a sauce or gravy, or coated first, they can be skinned. Certainly such ducks as goldeneyes, bluebills, and the sea ducks are better skinned. Skinning removes some of the fat and the strong flavor with it. Skinning game birds is very easy. Simply loosen the skin on the breast and start peeling. Skinning ducks is another matter. You have to pull and cut.

161

PLUCKING GAME BIRDS

Plucking game birds is a more time consuming chore, particularly if they have many pin feathers. Pluck the feathers out by taking "pinches" of them between the thumb and the first two fingers and pull with the grain — the direction in which they lie — not against the grain or you will tear the skin. Do not take pinches that are too big or the skin will tear. All game birds can be plucked dry. However, waterfowl, particularly if there are many of them, are much easier to pluck after being scalded for about twenty seconds in 145-degree water. The best way to scald the bird is to hold it by its head and dunk it into a bucket of scalding water. Waterfowl will have on them a hair-like fuzz. This is best removed by singeing with a candle. After plucking and dressing, the birds must be washed carefully and dried. They are then ready for the oven or the freezer.

Most game that has been shot cleanly and quickly and then properly handled after the shot will outclass anything you can buy in a supermarket. Game cooking is an art. A game dinner, fully complemented with side trimmings and fine wines, can be a feast indeed — a noble end to a good hunt.

Any outdoorsman may, at some time in his outdoor adventures, land or bag a trophy fish or animal. The procedures to follow in such a case are beyond the scope of this chapter on dealing with game and fish for the table. But there are many books on hunting and fishing that do deal with this.

Chapter 18

The ABC's of Wilderness Survival

Skills for wilderness survival, like those for administering first aid, are skills that every outdoorsman hopes he will never have to use. But when they are needed, they are indispensable. At the risk of sounding dramatic, they may spell the difference between life and death. I can only cover the very basic elements of wilderness survival in this chapter; the subject is simply too broad and complex.

A knowledge of wilderness survival is essential for anyone who loves to travel in the wilds — the aircraft carrying you into a remote fishing lake may crash; you may lose your compass and become lost; your canoe may overturn and all your gear may be lost. In short, an emergency may develop at any time. I don't think it is necessary for every outdoorsman to be a survival expert, but I do think that every outdoorsman should know the basics. Such skills, even if they are never used in an actual emergency, are helpful in building confidence and self reliance in the out-of-doors. A man who has confidence in his ability to survive in an emergency is unlikely to succumb to fear, loneliness, or panic.

Many excellent books have been written on the subject of wilderness survival, including one entitled *Wilderness Survival* by a good friend, Berndt Berglund. Even home-study courses in wilderness survival can be taken from National Survival Incorporated.

THE SEVEN DEADLY ENEMIES

To survive an emergency in the wilderness, you must be in the proper frame of mind. Your attitude — your determination to survive, the instinct to live — must be paramount. Fear, loneliness, pain, cold, fatigue, hunger, and thirst are the seven deadly enemies you must guard against. Singly or in combination, they can rob you of your self confidence or, even worse, of your desire to struggle for life.

Fear is nothing to be ashamed of. Only a fool is never afraid. The point is to control your fear and not let it get control of you. If the feeling of panic or fear starts to creep up on you, think of positive things — your ability as an outdoorsman, your skill in the woods. A man on the verge of panic cannot think logically. He is prone to rash actions that may be foolhardy and dangerous.

Loneliness is a second cousin to fear. They frequently travel together. The worst thing about loneliness is that it strikes without warning. Suddenly you realize that you are alone. This will gnaw at you, lowering your resistance and vitality. If you feel loneliness coming on, keep busy — sing, whistle to yourself, go out and gather food, do anything to keep your mind off the fact that you are alone.

Pain is nature's signal that something is wrong. In moments of excitement, you may not feel pain. But when things calm down a bit, pain surfaces. Tend to your wounds, but do not let pain get the best of you. It can weaken the desire to go on.

Cold can be a severe threat to survival. It numbs the spirit as well as the body. If you are out in the winter months, plan your shelter and fire in such a way as to minimize the effects of cold temperatures. A person freezes to death only when he is overly tired and sleepy; otherwise the cold will not let him fall asleep.

Fatigue reduces mental ability. It can make you thoughtless and uncaring. Fatigue is not always the result of overwork or overexertion. Many times it is the result of a mental attitude — frustration, hopelessness, or lack of a plan. Do not exert yourself, but keep making plans as to how to survive the crisis.

Hunger makes all of us more susceptible to cold, pain, and fear. A man with a full belly rarely loses his optimism. Conserve your food and, if you get a chance, add fish, game, and edible plants to your larder.

Thirst can be maddening. It can dull the mind and promote panic. A man can survive a week or longer without food, but not without water. In dry country, do not leave a water source. Beware of dehydration even when there is plenty of water around you.

TO STAY OR TO WALK OUT

Whether to stay and camp, or to attempt to walk out, is the first decision for you to make. If you are lost, you should stay. You do

---

◄*Smoke and fire are a good way to signal that you are lost. The signals should be in groups of three — the international distress signal. A "torch tree" is an excellent fire signal for passing aircraft.*

not know where to go anyway. That is why you are lost. Make camp near an opening or a lake where a searching aircraft will have a better chance of spotting you.

On the other hand, if you have been forced into a survival situation because of an airplane crash or a canoe overturning, you could attempt to walk out if you have a map and a compass and are not more than a few days from a road, a railway, or a human habitation. Otherwise you should stay. Do not risk getting lost. Searchers are more likely to find you if you are near an aircraft.

The first rule in a wilderness emergency is to keep your clothing and equipment in good repair. Your personal survival kit should contain a couple of needles and some strong thread. Mend any rips in your clothing. Sew on any buttons that may have come loose. Heated resin from evergreens makes good glue. Strips of green deer or moose hide make good bindings. As the hide dries, it will shrink and pull tighter. There is a way of repairing most clothing and tools in the wilderness — axes, knives, gunstocks, punctures in canoes, and so on — by using a bit of ingenuity.

SHELTERS

The first thing you must build is a shelter. What kind of shelter will depend on the materials at hand, including what material you may have with you. A shelter can be made from evergreen branches, bullrushes and reeds, sod, bark, slabs of rocks, or even snow blocks. Canvas or plastic sheeting are excellent.

A lean-to structure is the easiest to build. It should have at least a forty-five degree slope to its roof to shed rain. Roots or strips of bark or animal hide can be used as lashings. Do not make your shelter larger than necessary to hold you and your gear. The larger the shelter, the harder it will be to keep it warm. In cold weather, do not neglect to insulate the floor with evergreen boughs or, even better, with dry grass or rushes. Loose snow is an excellent insulating material for sides and roofs.

Do not neglect natural shelters such as caves, if they are not damp or occupied by bears. Spruce trees with branches to the ground can also make good snug shelters in winter. However, more branches may be needed to reinforce them. The only disadvantage with such shelters is that no fire can be built inside, lest it melt the snow. Snow houses are also potential shelters in the far north during winter, but a snow saw-knife is needed to build one. Only a downed aircraft would carry such an implement.

Shelters should be located in places that protect them from wind.

166

Summer may be the only exception to this because of insects. In summer, windswept areas have fewer blackflies and mosquitos. Remember, southern exposures are always warmer.

FIRE

Once a shelter has been built, a fire is an important consideration. To warm the shelter, build the fire as close to the opening of the shelter as safety will allow. Construct a log reflector behind the fire to reflect heat towards the shelter. If possible, use only dead, standing trees for firewood. These will be drier and will give better heat. Dead trees on the ground tend to be wet and burn poorly.

Make sure that you build a good fireplace of rocks or mineral soil so that your fire will not accidentally spread. A forest fire might leave you in an even worse predicament. In winter, do not build your fire near evergreen trees laden with snow. The heat may cause the snow to slide down. Shelter the fire from wind or build your fireplace on the lee side. Do not use rocks that might explode — limestone in particular — around a fire. Watch out for sparks and flying embers. They could burn holes in your clothing or sleeping bag.

Obviously anyone venturing into the bush, even if he is planning to stay on the fringes, should carry an ample supply of strike-anywhere matches in a waterproof container. In fact, I always carry two containers — the second one holding special wind-resistant and water-resistant matches. A cigarette lighter is also a good bet as long as the fuel lasts. I would not advise anyone going into the bush with only a lighter. A flint and steel should be a part of every personal survival kit.

Save your matches! This is one of the axioms of survival. Use tinder such as dry moss, grass, dry shredded cedar bark, or dry birch bark to start a fire. Have plenty of it on hand. If tinder is not handy, make feather sticks of dry soft wood for lighting fires. If you have a steel and flint in your survival kit, use it instead of matches. At night, bank your fire so that you can start a new one from the hot embers in the morning. This is an old Indian trick — it saves matches.

In an emergency, ammunition can be used to start a fire. How? It's easy. Simply remove the bullet or shot and wad from a round, and pour half the powder into a bed of tinder. Then place a bit of cotton, soft cloth, or dry moss or lichens into the round as wadding. Fire the gun in the air. The wadding should burst into flames and can then be placed on the tinder.

On sunny days, convex lenses such as magnifying glasses, miner's lenses, or lenses from cameras, rifle 'scopes, or binoculars can be used to start a fire by focusing the lens with a hot pinpoint on tinder. Film is also very highly flammable and a lens will ignite it almost immediately. A battery from a downed aircraft or wrecked power boat can produce an electric arc, and a gasoline-dampened rag or tinder will ignite instantly. But do not try this near the aircraft.

SIGNALS

There are a large number of signals that a lost person can use. Priority should be given to smoke signals. You may be in a wilderness area, but perhaps not so deep that a forest-fire tower or a fire-patrol aircraft cannot be able to spot you.

In a clearing, build three signal fires at least a hundred feet apart in a triangle. If this is not feasible because you are in thick bush, build three fires in a line or on a lakeshore or riverbank. These should be built near your shelter so that you can light them quickly if you hear an aircraft overhead. Build these fires from dry wood, but additional fuel should be green branches, moss, grass, or leaves — anything that will smoke heavily. Rubber and oil from aircraft make lots of black smoke. Do not try to keep the fires burning all the time or you will waste too much energy feeding them. But have the fires ready to start at a moment's notice. Keep the wood dry in case of bad weather by covering it with evergreen boughs. These can be burned later to create smoke.

Light signals are also effective. The best one is a "torch tree". It is visible for many miles. To do this, select a lone-standing evergreen with thick foliage. Dry, highly flammable material such as bark, kindling wood, or moss among the lower branches is necessary. Then build a big bonfire around the trunk of the tree at the base. As the bonfire flares up, it will ignite the tinder in the branches and start the entire tree burning like a huge torch.

Again, you should have the torch tree prepared ahead of time so that when you hear an aircraft you will be ready to signal. A torch tree can be started in the winter by knocking off all the snow and ice from the tree. If you start a couple of smaller fires near your intended torch tree, the heat from them will knock the snow off and help to dry the torch tree off. Torch trees throw sparks. So exhibit caution and vigilance against possible forest fires.

Gasoline and oil from a downed aircraft can be used to start a big flash fire when a search aircraft is used. A bed of grass or some cloth can be used for this gasoline-oil fire.

Three of anything — three shots, three whistle blasts, three flashes of a signal mirror — is the international distress code. This is the code you should use when signalling to searchers.

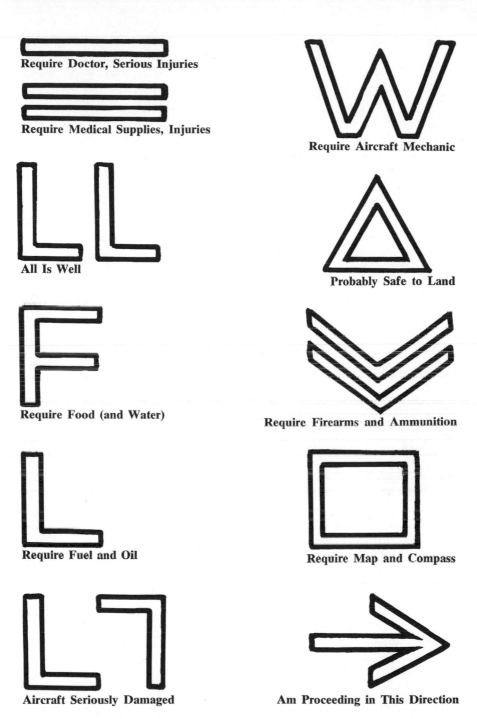

Require Doctor, Serious Injuries

Require Medical Supplies, Injuries

Require Aircraft Mechanic

All Is Well

Probably Safe to Land

Require Food (and Water)

Require Firearms and Ammunition

Require Fuel and Oil

Require Map and Compass

Aircraft Seriously Damaged

Am Proceeding in This Direction

Every outdoorsman who ventures into the wilderness should know the basic ground-to-air signals.

GROUND-TO-AIR SIGNALS

After you have prepared your smoke signals and torch tree, build some ground-to-air signals. These can be constructed from evergreen branches on snow or on a sandy beach. Peeled logs or white birch logs are good on a dark background. Sand, large rocks, and stones can also be used. The more contrast you can create between the signals and their background, the more easily they will be seen. Size is also important. They must be fifty feet long and longer if possible.

Be sure the terrain is reasonably safe for aircraft to land — that the lake is deep enough with no boulders, that there are no hidden rocks on the tundra, and that the terrain will support a light aircraft. If an aircraft cannot land, you may have to walk out.

FOOD AND WATER

A man with a full belly can withstand hardships that a starving man could never endure. Water is generally a problem only in dry country. A man lost in the deserts of the southwest or northern Mexico will be in serious trouble if he doesn't find water.

It is impossible for an uninjured, knowledgeable, and skilled outdoorsman to die of hunger in the temperate regions of this continent during the spring, summer, or autumn months. There is just too much food around. Even in winter, there is still plenty of food, but harvesting it is more difficult. Food is likely to be a more serious problem in the Arctic. But even here, a man with a rifle can survive.

The subject of food gathering — hunting, snaring, trapping, fishing, and harvesting edible plants and fruits — is so vast that I can only touch upon it in this chapter. However, I must state that there are very few creatures on this continent that a man should not eat, and certainly no fresh-water fish that are harmful.

If you ever become lost or stranded in the wilderness, immediately conserve any emergency rations you may have. If you can add to your food supply by harvesting any animals, fish, or edible plants, do so, even if you expect to be found or rescued the next day. Having an ample supply of food will give you confidence even if you are not rescued when expected. There is something about having a supply of food that is comforting to the human mind — a sort of hoarding instinct.

For example, I know a man who once got lost on a moose hunt. He was worried. From a high ridge he spotted a fairly large lake and decided that that was where he should stay while waiting to be found. On his way to the lake, he encountered a moose, which he promptly shot. After he dressed the moose and skinned it, keeping the hide intact to use as a blanket, he built a small lean-to against an overgrown tree near the shoreline of the lake. He built three smoke fires and waited. The second day after he was lost, he heard an aircraft. The aircraft spotted his smoke fires, landed on the lake, and rescued him. It even hauled out his quartered moose. The man was at no time worried about not surviving. He knew that he had enough food for a long time and this gave him the confidence he needed to settle down and wait to be rescued.

EDIBLE PLANTS

Green plants such a spruce tips, willow tips, leaves of Labrador tea, dandelion leaves, and many others are a good source of Vitamin C. The best way to ingest this is to drink tea made from such leaves. Rose hips, the fruits of the wild rose, also have a high Vitamin C content. Another good source of Vitamin C is the cambium, the inner layer between the bark and the wood of poplar, jack pine, and spruce.

The flowers of many wild plants in North America are safe to eat. The roots of cattail, wild carrot, tiger lily, lady's slipper, arrowhead plant, vetch, and other plants with thick fibrous roots are good sources of carbohydrates. They can be eaten raw or boiled. The roots of the water lily are edible when boiled twice or even three times, but the water should be changed between boilings to remove the acrid flavor.

Greens such as dandelion leaves, young green milkweed pods, young waterlily seed pods, the lower inner core of young cattails, and young pigweed can all be eaten raw or stewed. Fiddleheads, the fronds of ferns, are delicious.

Berries are another source of food. Almost everyone knows the common ones such as blueberries, raspberries, blackberries, cranberries, and wintergreen. But be careful with others unless you can positively identify them. Red and white berries are more prone to be poisonous than not, unless you know them. Avoid any black or blue-colored berries in bunches. If you come across berries you don't know and want to try them, eat only a few and wait twenty-four hours for a reaction. Then eat a little more and wait again. If, after the second twenty-four-hour period, nothing unpleasant has occurred, the berries are probably safe. Other fruits such as wild cherries, acorns, and nuts of all kinds are safe to eat.

Among the lower plants, lichens can be eaten. Scrape these off rocks and stumps. They can be eaten boiled, dried, or dried and powdered, and used in stews and soups. The lemon lichen is edible and very common. Mushrooms should be eaten only by those who know them. Although only a few are poisonous, these can be deadly. Generally speaking, anything that birds and animals eat is likely to be safe for you to eat, but always make the sample-and-wait test before eating something new or unknown. Two very poisonous plants are the baneberry with its cluster of red and white berries and the water hemlock whose purple-streaked leaves have a foul odor when crushed. There are no poisonous plants above the tree line in the Arctic.

The water hemlock is one of the relatively few poisonous plants in the out-doors. Other deadly plants include some of the mushrooms and the bane-berry.

WILDLIFE

Aside from some of the insects, particularly caterpillars, you can eat just about anything in the way of animal life. Large earthworms, snails, grasshoppers, and crickets are all edible. Grasshoppers or locusts have a nutty flavor when roasted, and are considered a delicacy in the Middle East. Frogs, lizards, and snakes (even the poisonous ones) can also be eaten. Indeed, snakes are reputed to be quite tasty.

However, mammals, birds, and fish are generally more important to a man trying to survive, if for no other reason than because they are larger and more abundant. While plant materials and some of the invertebrate animals can be gathered with the bare hands, this is not the case for fish, birds, and mammals. You will have to have or make traps, snares, or weapons. Snares and traps are the most effect-

ive way of taking small mammals and birds. Rabbits can be easily taken by snares of different types. The snares should be set on known rabbit runs. These are easy to find in thick cover or when snow is on the ground. Squirrels can also be taken on snares set on leaning poles against trees. It is wise to set two or three snares in succession, because often squirrels travel in pairs.

Big game such as deer can also be snared. There are essentially two types of snares for this. One is the Apache foot snare which snares the animal's foot and is anchored to a log which the animal must drag. The other is a neck or head snare set about eighteen inches off the ground. The noose must be about twenty-four inches in diameter. This snare is also anchored to a log or a very strong whippy sapling. These snares must be set on known deer trails.

Snares can be made of almost any kind of rope or wire. Certainly wire snares are superior to anything else because they are thin, difficult to see, and easy to bend into position. For big game, the snare has to be very strong because a snared animal will exert a great deal of force in its frenzy to get away. Snares for small game can be made from strips of deer skin or moose hide, strong string, or heavy fishing line. I have even used boot laces. Most small game snares are lethal. They kill the animal almost instantly. Every survival kit should contain a coil or two of snare wire.

Snares, when properly set on game trails, can be used to capture a wide range of animals.

Fur-bearing animals such as foxes can be taken with a stone bee-hive trap baited with fish. Dead-fall traps can also be used. Birds can be caught in the Ojibway bird snare. The Canada jay or whiskeyjack is particularly vulnerable. Gulls can be caught on baited fish hooks. Grouse — ruffed, blue, and spruce — can frequently be caught on a noose on a pole. Indeed, often grouse can be killed with rocks. In the wilderness, these birds are usually very trusting. The eggs and young of birds are very nutritious. Nests of ground-nesting birds are easy to find on the Arctic islands. Geese can be killed with clubs during their flightless stage of moult.

Generally mammals cannot be taken without a weapon. A club is the easiest weapon to make. A club is all a man needs for a porcupine. A rap on the head will kill this spiny animal instantly. A porcupine should be skinned from its bare belly. If you see porcupine damage on the branches of trees, watch carefully. You will probably en-counter more porcupines in trees, and they are easily shaken down.

The only other mammals that can be killed with a club are lem-mings and mice. Lemmings in particular may be a very important source of survival food in the Arctic regions. Such aquatic mammals as beavers and muskrats are also easily killed with a club, if you can catch them on shore. If you see beaver activity, watch carefully. Sit down and wait. Perhaps you can catch one by cutting off its escape route once it goes on land.

Other simple weapons are: throwing sticks for birds and small mammals, a catapult made from any rubber or elastic in an aircraft, or even a bow and arrow. But usually these weapons are not very effective and practice is needed with them to achieve a fair degree of proficiency.

A firearm is invaluable for survival. Normally aircraft flying over wilderness areas carry guns in their survival kits. In hunting for sur-vival, one must forget any sort of sporting ethic. Your ability to sur-vive depends on your skill as a hunter. The man who knows inti-mately the habits and habitat requirements of wildlife is bound to be more successful as a hunter. The basic rules of hunting are: move quietly and slowly; look a lot; move upwind or cross wind; watch for game signs such as well-worn game trails, tracks, droppings, feed-ing activities, dens, holes, and salt licks. In dry country, water holes are good places to wait downwind.

Remember that any bird or mammal can be eaten — even such fur-bearing animals as mink, martens, fishers, foxes and wolves. The various ground squirrels, marmots, and woodchucks are all edible. Such animals as otters, lynx, bobcat, and cougar have a reputation of being very tasty. Owls are said to be indistinguishable from grouse in a stew pot.

176

Remember not to waste ammunition. Kill the biggest animal you can find. Deer, elk, moose, and bears are all very good to eat. So are seal, caribou, muskox, and polar bear in the Arctic regions. Any sort of firearm is better than none. In an emergency, game can be killed with a shotgun loaded with bird shot if the hunter can get close enough. Big game can also be killed with a small-bore rifle such as the common .22 rimfire. However, center-fire rifles of .30 caliber are the best choice for big game animals, while a twelve-gauge shotgun is the most efficient type of firearm for small game.

A Mauser-type bolt-action rifle is an excellent choice for an aircraft and for wilderness expeditions because of its simplicity, ruggedness, and dependability. The well-known .30, 06 caliber is probably the wisest choice. A double-barrelled shotgun with two triggers is the best type of shotgun. It is rugged and simple, it can be dismantled readily to fit into a small place and, above all, it is really two guns in one. Should the firing pin break on one barrel, the other barrel can still be used. Also, one barrel of such a gun can be loaded with bird shot for small game while the other barrel can be loaded with rifle slugs or buckshot for big game. The hunter is then prepared for any type of game he may encounter.

Another excellent survival firearm is the combination over-and-under. With such a gun one barrel is a rifle barrel and the other is a shotgun. The combination over-and-unders are made in many different rifle calibers and shotgun gauges in Europe, including .30, 06 and twelve gauge. Unfortunately these guns are very expensive — $500 or more. However, there is a suitable over-and-under made in the United States — the Savage Model 24V. This is available in .30-30 and twenty gauge, three-inch magnum barrels. The twenty-gauge magnum comes close to being as effective as a twelve gauge. The .30-30 cartridge is not as good as the .30, 06 for very big game such as moose and elk, but it is ample if a hunter gets close enough and places his shot well. The advantage of an over-and-under is that one firearm is both a rifle and a shotgun. The Savage Model 24V is a simple, rugged gun, and at the same time it is short and light. It can be taken down for storage. Its current list price is a little less than $100.

Fish can be an important source of food. During spawning runs in the spring or fall, many species of fish — pike, trout, char, salmon, and suckers — are particularly vulnerable. Dams of various kinds can be constructed in the shallows to trip or contain the fish. They are also more vulnerable to spearing and snagging at this time. A surprisingly efficient fish spear can be made from a tri-fork of a green hardwood limb that has been baked in a fire to harden. The points should be sharp and, if possible, have barbs.

Of course fish can also be caught on hooks and line. Certainly every personal survival kit should have strong line, hooks of various sizes, and some artificial lures such as spoons and spinners. Hooks can also be fashioned from nails, pins, animal bones, and shells. Metal can be heated in a fire and crude hooks pounded and bent with stones.

Lures can be fashioned from shiny metal. The bowl of a soup spoon makes a very fine fishing spoon once a hook is attached. Brightly colored bits of cloth and bits of aluminum foil can also be used as lures. Meat of any kind, particularly the less edible parts of fish, and, of course, large insects, frogs, crawfish, and earthworms all make suitable bait.

An aircraft should carry a good length of fishing net — nylon gill-net being best — fully equipped with sinkers and floats. Fishing with a net is far more effective than fishing with a hook and line. Once the net is set, it works continuously. A net can be set just about anywhere, including under the ice, by being passed from one hole to another with notched sticks. The places to set a net are near steep drop-offs, entrances of weedy bays, stream mouths, and pools below rapids — in short, the kind of places that fish frequent.

COOKING AND PRESERVING MEAT

My first piece of advice is not to waste anything. Almost every part of an animal can be eaten except the bones and hair. Aside from such internal organs as the liver, heart, and kidneys, other parts such as the lungs, stomach, intestines, and brain can all be eaten. (Only the liver from the polar bear is poisonous because of its high vitamin A content.) The long bones of legs can be cracked open for their nourishing marrow. Do not waste any fat, even if you cannot eat it now. You may need it later to eat with lean meat such as rabbits. Fat may also be used to make leather boots waterproof and to soften dry skins.

Do not waste any skins or hides. When you skin an animal, do it in such a way that the skin remains intact. The skins can be used for blankets, coverings, clothing, or for making into rope.

Game and fish can be cooked in a number of ways. If you have a large survival kit from an aircraft, no doubt it will contain cooking utensils. The task of cooking is much easier then. But game and fish can be cooked over an open fire by broiling it on a green stick over the coals and flames. This is probably the best way to cook small game, birds, and fish. Chunks of moose or caribou meat or chunks of a big fish can also be cooked in this way.

Strips of meat can also be cooked directly on coals or on any sheets of metal placed on the coals. Fish can be split open and attached to a slab of a log and cooked that way. Both fish and meat can be baked in hot coals by coating the fish or meat in clay. The scales or skin should be left attached to the fish. Do not eat any fish raw because of parasites, but deer, moose, and caribou can certainly be eaten rare like beef. However, bear meat should be cooked well like pork and for the same reason — it can cause trichinosis when eaten raw.

Meat and fish can be preserved in a number of ways. Freezing is the simplest. But they can also be cut into thin strips and fillets and dried in the sun and wind or over a smoky fire. Large chunks of meat can be preserved in coolish weather simply by hanging them in a cool, dry, and breezy spot and letting a hard crust or rind form around them. This rind is cut away when the meat is eaten. Moisture is the big culprit behind meat spoilage. If a mold forms on the outside of moist meat, cut or scrape the mold away and eat the meat. The mold is just a fungus. In warm weather cooked meat of any sort keeps better than raw meat.

Smoking is a very effective way of preserving meat. A simple smoke house can be built on a steep bank. Just dig a trench up the bank and cover it with branches and sod. The fireplace is at the bottom of the trench. A shelter or smoke chamber is constructed in the form of a tepee at the top using bark, skins, canvas, or sticks covered with sod. The smoke will travel up the trench into the smoke chamber.

Hardwoods are the best bet as far as woods used for smoking are concerned. If possible, avoid evergreen which, due to their gums and resins, have a tendency to give the meat an oil-flavour. In the Arctic, permafrost provides good cold storage. Dig a hole until you hit it. Put your meat in, preferably wrapped in something, and bury it.

Surplus food should be stored or cached so that it is safe from would-be robbers — mice, birds, and bears. Hanging meat ten to fifteen feet off the ground will protect it from bears but, unless it is covered, Canada jays and even ravens will get at it. Evergreen branches can be hung around it to ward off at least some birds.

SURVIVAL KITS

Throughout this chapter I have frequently referred to survival kits. I do not think anyone should go on a wilderness trip, even for a day, without some essential pieces of survival equipment. Ideally this equipment should be contained in a canvas or leather pouch. The personal survival kit must be light enough and small enough to fit into the pocket of a jacket or on a belt.

It should contain a small folding knife, a small compass, a signalling mirror, a whistle for signalling, fishing line, hooks, three or four lures, snare wire, a waterproof container of strike-anywhere matches, a flint and steel for starting fires, a container of waterproof and wind-resistant matches, two cubes of chemical fire starter in case no dry tinder can be found, needles and strong thread, and a couple of sticks of freeze-dried meat or salami. Besides this the outdoorsman should carry on his person a good knife plus a fairly sophisticated compass and a small pocket stone in a leather sheath for touching up the knife's edge.

A survival kit for an aircraft should contain a personal kit along the lines mentioned above, plus a firearm and ammunition, an ax, a folding shovel, emergency rations (canned or freeze-dried), cooking utensils, tough plastic sheeting or a piece of canvas for shelter. All this should be in a kit bag or duffel bag. The aircraft should also carry sleeping bags plus a small tent.

FILE A FLIGHT PLAN

Just as aircraft file flight plans on where they are going, so should you. No one should ever venture into the wilderness without telling someone, preferably two or more people, where they are going and when they will be back.

If you are hiking, hunting, or fishing in the wilderness out of the main camp, tell your partners in which direction you are going. Arrange a signal — three shots or a signal flare fired from a rifle — for a specific hour at night if one of you fails to return by nightfall. If you are going on a wilderness canoe trip, tell the forest ranger or local game warden when you expect to be back, with instructions that if you are two days late to organize a search.

If you are camped alone somewhere and are going out for a day's hike, leave a note at your campsite telling where you are going and when you expect to be back. If you have driven to a spot to fish or hike for a day, leave a note on your car windshield.

File a personal flight plan. It can save your life.

Chapter 19

The Outdoorsman's First-Aid Kit

The old Boy Scout motto — Be Prepared — may sound like a corny cliché but its meaning is still very applicable to every outdoorsman. No one should go on a canoe trip, a fishing trip, or a camping trip without an adequate first-aid kit and, of course, some knowledge of first aid.

There are many first-aid kits on the market for use in an automobile. Some are simply junk, but others are well conceived and equipped. The better kits are ideal for an automobile camping trip, but they are too bulky and heavy for the backpacker, the canoe tripper, the hiker, or even the hunter or fisherman going on a fly-in or horseback trip.

Here is a plan for a first-aid kit that is light enough and small enough to be packed along on any wilderness trip, yet it can be used to treat everything from a fairly serious cut to dysentery. This kit was designed by E. Russell Kodet, M.D., and was described in *Outdoor Life* magazine some years ago. I have assembled one of these kits and have found it to be extremely useful. Some of the contents have yet to be used, but a day may come when they will be needed.

There is no substitute for immediate medical attention when a serious injury has occurred. But on wilderness trips, medical attention is generally hours, if not days, away. And even on outings near hospitals and doctors, immediate first aid can minimize discomfort and pain and even prevent death.

Now for the kit. The only liquid that this kit contains is eyedrops. Liquids are heavy and they frequently spill. There is also no alcohol or antiseptic in this kit. Although many first-aid books, particularly the older ones, recommend that cuts and scratches be doused liberally with alcohol or antiseptics to kill germs, these materials also kill living tissue. Germs grow best in dead or devitalized tissue, and certainly devitalized tissue heals more slowly than healthy tissue.

The best way to treat cuts and scratches is to wash them with soap and water and dress them. If the wound is oozing, a plastic-like absorbent tissue such as Telfa should be placed over the wound first to prevent sticking. Then the wound should be dressed. The gauze recommended for this kit is the Kling type. This gauze adheres to itself, thereby making it easier to use. A gaping wound should be brought together with a "butterfly" plastic tape. In areas where there is a fair amount of movement, a butterfly may not do the job. A suture may be needed. No one should attempt sutures — even if he knows how — if the victim can be taken to a doctor. But if a doctor is days away, there may be no other choice. Making a stitch or suture is not difficult. Since the wound is generally painful already and the nerves lying close to the skin are frequently severed by the cut, the needle causes less pain than one might suspect. No pain killers such as Novocaine are used, because syringes and needles require special precautions that just don't fit into the scheme of a first-aid kit such as this.

Suturing packages can be bought with the needle already attached to the suture material. They come in different thicknesses, but 3-0 is suitable for everything except the face. The cut should be washed and dried, and then stitched. The needle is held in a hemostat, a sort of small, medical, needle-nosed plier that locks. The hemostat has other uses in the wilderness as well, such as removing thorns and slivers.

Stitches should always be taken only through the skin, never deeper. After the knot is tied the ends are left one-quarter inch long to make removal (after about seven days) easier. No suturing should ever be attempted near the eyes by a layman. The one advantage of suturing is that it usually stops the bleeding very quickly, and this makes the injured person feel much more at ease.

Eyedrops that will act as a local anesthetic and treat inflammation or infection can be very useful on a wilderness trip. An outdoorsman's eyes are very susceptible to injury. A branch can whip back and hit him in the face; wood chips from chopping wood present a hazard; cinders from a campfire are hazardous; and snow blindness can occur from participation in winter sports such as snowshoeing, ski touring, snowmobiling, ice fishing, or hunting in winter. In high altitudes, one can get conjunctivitis which has symptoms like snow blindness. One good eyedrop remedy is a mixture of equal parts of Pontocaine and Neohydeltrasol. A drop every two or three hours is the recommended dosage. The treated eye will lose its ability to blink, which protects and cleanses it from dust, so cover it with a clean handkerchief or at least stay out of windy places. This will wear off in approximately two hours.

Hikers, backpackers, and hunters going into the mountains frequently get headaches due to the high altitude, but after the first day or two they usually adjust to the thinner air. Aspirin can be taken for headache relief, but often it is not enough. An Empirin compound is more effective. This can also be used to relieve pain due to sunburn, poison-ivy rash, or sprains. It has no effect on pain stemming from internal organs.

Nausea and intestinal cramps can be treated with Tridol or Campazine. The dosage rates vary depending on the weight of the tablets; a dozen tablets should be ample. If continuous vomiting occurs, get medical help fast. It could be something serious.

For severe infections, blood poisoning, and pneumonia, strong antibiotics are needed. The kit should contain penicillin or Achromycin. Ten tablets should be ample. But you must be careful with penicillin. Some persons are allergic to it, and treating someone with penicillin who does not know whether or not he is allergic can be hazardous.

Diarrhoea can also be a problem, particularly when traveling in the wilderness of Africa or South America. Tainted foods or water are frequent causes of this. Lomotil tablets give relief. Eighteen tablets should be ample for any emergency. Sulfasuxidine is also good for sterilizing the intestines. The kit should include some tablets for relief of constipation, which can be caused by a change in diet.

If you have any recurring health problems, the kit should contain necessary medication to treat it. This should be spare medication in excess of what you will need.

Many of the drugs I have suggested can be obtained only with a doctor's prescription, so consult with your family physician. Most family doctors will give you the necessary prescriptions once they know what these drugs are to be used for. It is not a bad idea to consult him about the contents of your first-aid kit. He may have valuable suggestions. Some doctors may have trepidations about some of the treatments (for example, the suturing), but when they realize that you would stitch a victim only when you are four days of hard paddling away from medical help, they will see the point

The kit I have suggested costs about twenty dollars to assemble. It weighs no more than six ounces including the pouch that it is kept in. If you make substitutions in the kit, keep weight and bulk in mind.

The following is a list of the proposed contents of a first-aid kit:

    Band Aids
    gauze flats
    Kling roller bandage
    butterflies
    tape

suture packages
hemostat
scalpel blades (or small scissors)
nausea and cramp tablets
dysentery and anti-constipation tablets
antibiotics
Empirin compound
eyedrops

Chapter 20

First Aid in the Outdoors

Everyone should know a bit of first aid, but such knowledge is even more essential for an outdoorsman who frequently is far from a hospital or doctor. Knowing what to do when a calamity strikes could ease pain or suffering, and even prevent death.

The basic techniques for first aid are simple. There is no reason for not knowing them. With a little knowledge of first aid and a first-aid kit such as the one described in the previous chapter, you can handle most minor mishaps.

GENERAL RULES

Whether treating a victim of an accident or illness, there are several basic rules you must follow in administering first aid. They are:

1. Remain calm. Carry out your first-aid tasks quickly, quietly, and with an absolute minimum of fuss and panic.

2. Check the breathing of the victim. Give artificial respiration if breathing has stopped. With this procedure, every second counts.

3. Check bleeding. Do not touch burns or injuries with your bare hands.

4. Do not move the patient unless you are certain he can be moved safely.

5. Reassure the patient and keep him calm, warm, and comfortable.

6. Do not administer liquids to an unconscious person.

7. Watch for symptoms of shock.

8. Do not attempt too much. Do the minimum that is essential to save life and to prevent the condition from worsening; but remember, you are only a layman.

There are two types of afflictions that can mar an outdoor trip — accidents and illnesses. The following will give you a brief idea of what to do in the case of the more common types of accidents and illnesses. There are several good books available on general first-aid procedures, one of which is put out by the St. John Ambulance Association, the volunteer first-aid organization.

ACCIDENTS

Cuts, Scrapes, Abrasions These types of wounds are fairly common in the outdoors, resulting from falls, misuse of knives, and so on. What generally has to be done in these cases is to stop the bleeding and prevent any infection. Make the patient sit or lie down. Blood escapes with far less force when the patient sits quietly, and still less force when the patient is prone. Elevate the bleeding part, except in the case of a fractured limb. It is important to remember not to remove any blood clot that has already formed. Remove any foreign bodies that are visible in the wound and around it, by picking or wiping these off with a piece of clean dressing. Apply and maintain pressure until the bleeding stops. Apply a dressing pad and a bandage.

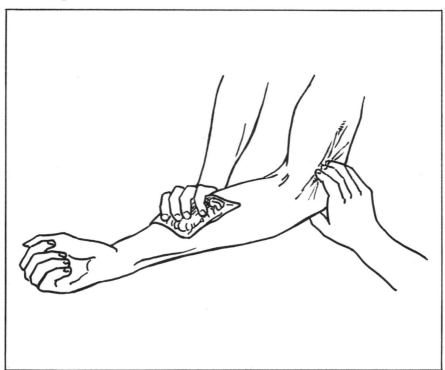

In the case of lacerations stop the bleeding as quickly as possible by applying hand pressure above the wound; then apply a dressing pad.

In the case of very severe lacerations, a constrictive bandage, such as a tourniquet, may have to be used to stop or retard hemorrhaging. Be sure to loosen the bandage every fifteen minutes so that the remainder of the limb receives an adequate supply of blood.

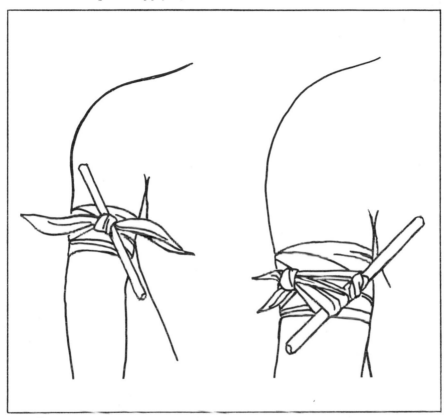

In the case of hemorrhage, pressure will have to be applied to the part of the wound from which the blood is coming. If a foreign body or a broken bone is present in the wound, press alongside it and not over it. Dress the wound and continue the application of pressure until the bleeding stops.

Fractures The most important thing to remember with a fracture is to treat it on the spot. You should never try to move the casualty until the fractured part has been immobilized, unless, of course, the life of the patient is in danger from some other cause. If circumstances dictate that final immobilization cannot be completed on the spot, then sufficient temporary immobilization should be carried out so that the patient can be moved safely to another location. Generally speaking, hemorrhages and severe wounds should be dealt with before fractures.

187

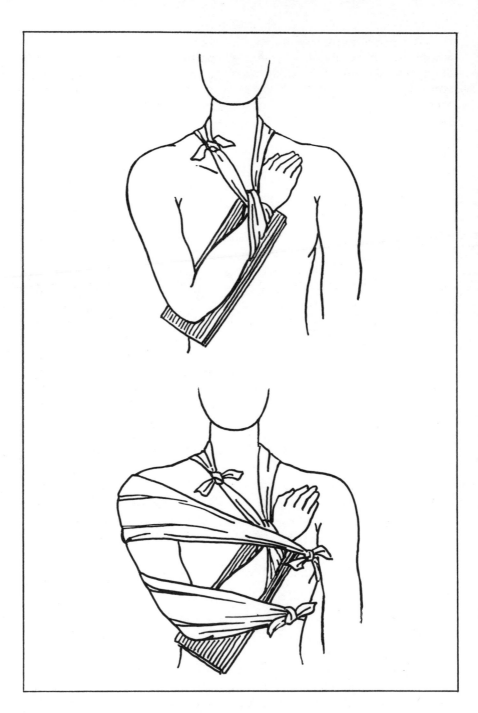

Fractures should be immobilized on the spot with the use of bandages and splints so that no further movement of broken bones will occur.

Fractures can be immobilized by the use of bandages and splints. Be careful when applying either of these — there may be more than one broken bone involved. Bandages must be applied firmly enough to prevent harmful movement, but they must not be so tight as to prevent blood circulation. In the case of a broken limb, swelling may occur and then the bandages will become too tight. If this happens, loosen them.

Splints should be long enough to immobilize the joint both above and below the fracture. They must be firm and preferably wide and they should also be well padded. Splints can be improvised from staffs, ski poles, pieces of wood, or even from stiff cardboard. Once the fractured limb has been immobilized the patient should be moved out very carefully to medical help.

Burns It is important when treating burns to avoid handling the affected areas any more than necessary. Always make sure that your hands are as clean as possible. Do not apply lotions of any kind. Do not remove burnt clothing, and do not break any blisters that may form. Cover the burn with a prepared, dry, sterile dressing from your first-aid kit. You can bandage the burned area firmly while seeking medical help, but if there are blisters present on the burn, bandage only lightly.

Sunburn All outdoorsmen like to get out in the hot summer sun, but watch out for sunburn! Prevention is the best cure for sunburn. Sunburn is treated in much the same way as other burns. If the sunburn is severe, an antiseptic emulsion can be applied freely and covered with a dressing or bandage. Leave the dressing on. Do not break any blisters that may form. And remember, sunburn can also occur on a bright day in winter.

Windburn Windburn can also be a problem in the out-of-doors. It can be treated in much the same way as sunburn, but it, too, can be prevented by wearing proper clothing and by covering exposed areas of flesh with a lotion or cream to prevent the skin from drying out on windy days.

Heat Exhaustion, Heat Stroke, and Sun Stroke All are very serious if you are far away from medical help. The best treatment for all of these is to place the patient in the coolest spot possible, to remove his clothing, and to sprinkle him with water or wrap him in a wet sheet and fan him. The idea here is to lower his body temperature. But take care not to lower the temperature too much. When the temperature has been lowered, wrap the patient in a dry sheet and continue to fan him. If his temperature rises again, repeat the treatment. In the case of heat exhaustion, the patient may complain of feeling cold. If he does, keep him comfortably warm. Watch his body temperature carefully.

Heart Attacks It is very difficult, if not impossible, for first-aid laymen to tell if a person who becomes faint or unconscious is suffering from a heart attack. If you are going into the outdoors with someone who is known to have a heart condition, he will probably have medication with him. Find out beforehand where his medication is kept and what the dosages are.

In the case of a suspected heart attack, move the patient as little as possible. Support him in a sitting position, as a failing heart works more economically this way than lying down. Be careful not to let him fall forward. Also, undo any tight clothing around the neck or waist to lessen any impediment to blood circulation or breathing. Get the patient medical aid as soon as you can.

Frostbite   Frostbite and freezing are dangerous because they may become extensive before you are fully aware of them. If you engage in a lot of winter sports, you should be on the alert for freezing.

As soon as frostbite is recognized, thaw the frostbitten area by applying heat. For frostbite spots on the face, a warm hand will sometimes suffice. Make certain the area is dry. Do not rub or massage the frostbitten area. This may cause the tissues that are fragile when frozen to break. Do not apply snow. Because snow is at air temperature, it will only make the frostbite worse.

If a hand or foot is frozen, warm it very gradually, and in the meantime, massage the parts adjacent to the frostbitten area so that circulation will be increased. The patient can drink warm fluids, but you must be careful not to apply any heat directly to the frozen part. After thawing has taken place, an antiseptic emulsion can be applied and the area can be bandaged. Swelling, redness, and most likely blistering will occur sometime after the frostbitten part has been thawed. Get the patient to a doctor as soon as possible.

Snowblindness   Snowblindness is becoming increasingly frequent due to the growing popularity of winter sports such as snowmobiling, snowshoeing, and cross-country skiing. Snowblindness is literally a "burning" of the eyes caused by light reflected in all directions from snow. Treatment consists mainly of shielding the eyes from light. Put a bandage around the eyes and get the victim to medical aid as soon as possible. The victim will probably need an opthalmic ointment and a week or more of care to cure his eyes. Incidentally, people who have suffered from snowblindness before are more susceptible to it.

Blisters   Blisters are one of the medical scourges of the outdoors. Every outdoorsman, at one time or another, gets a blister on his foot from a pair of boots that just do not agree with him. The best way to avoid blisters is to wear comfortable boots and good socks. Make sure your boots are well broken in before going on long hikes or trips. If blisters do occur, do not break them. Keep them bandaged with dry sterile gauze and let them dry up on their own.

190

Shock Shock is a condition of severe depression of the vital functions. It can occur in conjunction with most of the afflictions mentioned above. Shock is generally associated with changes in the circulatory system, mainly due to loss of whole blood or plasma. The severity of shock depends on the amount and rapidity of the blood loss. When treating any of the conditions mentioned above, always watch for signs of shock. General symptoms of shock may vary from a transient attack of faintness to a complete state of collapse. General signs include giddiness and faintness, coldness, nausea, pallor, cold clammy skin, a slow pulse rate which tends to become progressively worse, vomiting, and unconsciousness.

Shock is treated by laying the victim on his back with his head low and turned to one side (unless there is an injury to the head or chest). Reassure the patient and loosen clothing about the neck, chest, and waist. Wrap him in something warm. If he complains of thirst, give him sips of water, tea, or some other liquid, but no alcohol. Do not apply heat or friction to the limbs. Get the patient to a doctor as soon as possible.

ILLNESSES

Illnesses are not very often encountered in the out-of-doors. Perhaps the most common ones are diarrhoea and constipation due to change of habits and change of food. Any first-aid kit should contain medication to combat either of these afflictions, but if the conditions persist, the patient should go to a doctor.

Nausea can occur on canoeing or boating trips to people who are prone to seasickness. If you are prone to seasickness, take along some anti-nausea pills (available in any pharmacy).

People who suffer from hayfever or other allergies sometimes have problems in the outdoors during the late summer and early fall because of the amount of weed pollen in the air. People with known allergies should carry their prescribed medications with them.

Anyone going on a trip into the outdoors who has a particular medical problem should make certain that he has enough prescribed medication with him for the trip and in case of possible emergency. If you have any medications that should be taken at specific times or for specific purposes, let your outdoor partner know about them.

A knowledge of first aid is particularly important in the out-of-doors because so often medical help is a fair distance away. But the most important thing to remember on your outdoor adventures is the old cliché about an ounce of prevention being worth more than a pound of cure.

In this book, I have tried to pass on many of the elemental skills and some of the basic know-how that everyone who ventures into the outdoors should have. Some sections have dealt only with pleasures and esthetics, others have dealt with practical knowledge, and some are for emergency use only.

But equally important, I have tried to give a glimpse, a basic insight, into the rational use of the outdoors. There are times when it is just as wrong to lead a string of pack-horses over a mountain meadow as it is to shoot a bull elk. But there are times when both can be done without nature being the loser. The real outdoorsman knows the right and the wrong things, the right and wrong times.